100 DAYS of ADVENTURE

NATURE ACTIVITIES, CREATIVE PROJECTS, and FIELD TRIPS for EVERY SEASON

GRETA ESKRIDGE

ILLUSTRATED BY EMILY PAIK

Tommy NELSON®

An Imprint of Thomas Nelson

ISBN 978-1-4002-3099-0 (Paperback)
ISBN 978-1-4002-3098-3 (eBook)

Library of Congress Cataloging-in-Publication Data

Names: Eskridge, Greta, 1976- author. | Paik, Emily, illustrator.
Title: 100 days of adventure: nature activities, creative projects, and field trips for every season / Greta Eskridge; illustrated by Emily Paik.
Description: Nashville, TN: Tommy Nelson; Thomas Nelson, [2022] | Audience: Ages: 6–10 | Summary: "This colorful book of hands-on activities for children will connect and enrich your family through adventures, small and big. In 100 Days of Adventure by Greta Eskridge, kids ages 6 to 10 will learn about nature, art, music, and themselves through outdoor and indoor explorations, experiments, crafts, recipes, and more"—Provided by publisher.
Identifiers: LCCN 2021033342 (print) | LCCN 2021033343 (ebook) | ISBN 9781400230990 (paperback) | ISBN 9781400230983 (epub)
Subjects: LCSH: Amusements—Juvenile literature. | Recreation—Juvenile literature. | Nature study—Juvenile literature. | Handicraft for children—Juvenile literature.
Classification: LCC GV1203 .E78 2022 (print) | LCC GV1203 (ebook) | DDC 790—dc23
LC record available at https://lccn.loc.gov/2021033342
LC ebook record available at https://lccn.loc.gov/2021033343

Images used with permission from Greta Eskridge.

Additional images used under license by Shutterstock.

Printed in Thailand

22 23 24 25 26 IMG 6 5 4 3 2

Mfr: Imago / Thailand / February 9, 2022 / PO #12034411

TO ALL MY ADVENTURE BUDDIES—
EXPLORING WITH YOU IS MY FAVORITE PART OF THE
WEEK! I LOVE WHEN YOU SHOW ME YOUR DISCOVERIES
AND WHEN YOU COME SEE MINE. THANK YOU FOR
ENJOYING THIS WONDERFUL WORLD WITH ME.
I LOOK FORWARD TO HAVING AT LEAST ONE
HUNDRED MORE ADVENTURES TOGETHER!

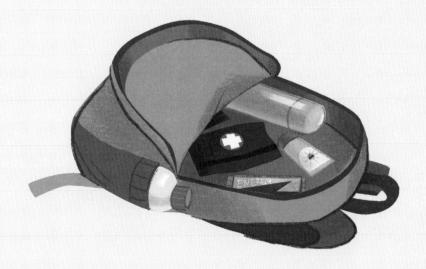

CONTENTS

SUMMER

FALL

WINTER

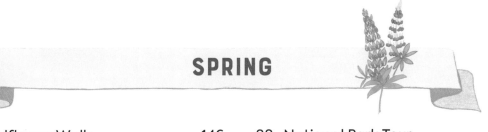

SPRING

NOTE TO PARENTS

This book is an invitation. It's an invitation to your child to say yes to adventure. But more than that, it's an invitation to you to say yes to creating connection between your child and you—and between your child and the real, exciting, wonderful world. It's an invitation for you to adventure together.

The truth is that we live in a time when there are so many things vying for our children's attention and, even more, for their hearts. There is an endless array of activities to take part in, technology to get lost in, and the societal need to keep up with what everyone else is doing. These things can create distance between our hearts and the hearts of our kids. Adventuring with your child offers the opportunity to draw close by creating time and space for building your relationship. Adventures provide a dedicated time together to talk, grow, laugh, and learn—and to make memories, which is the stuff lasting connections are made of.

One of my favorite things about going on adventures with my kids is that we're not going through the day on autopilot. We are fully engaged with the world around us and with one another. Adventures get us outside our normal routine, and every part of us feels the impact. Change engages all our senses: we see new things, smell new aromas, taste new foods, hear new sounds, and feel new things physically and emotionally.

This is incredibly important to me because all of us are becoming less and less engaged with nature, books, creativity, and face-to-face relationships. I want my kids to feel the pull of those real, tangible experiences and choose to engage with them. I want my kids to smile and say hello to strangers on a trail instead of always looking down at a screen. I want them to look up and see a hawk soaring overhead or notice the way thunderheads are forming over the mountains. I want them to get lost in a story we are reading together instead of getting lost in the bottomless scroll of social media. I want my kids to be changed by the amazing world we live in and the beauty, people, and ideas they encounter in it. But that will happen only if we get out and experience the world. It will happen only if we say yes to adventure!

—GRETA ESKRIDGE

ADVENTURES FOR SUMMER

BECOME A BACKYARD NATURALIST

THE PERFECT PET

THE SHOW MUST GO OUT

ALL TIED UP

TAKE A HIKE

NATURE'S SWIMMING POOLS

ON THE ROAD

INSECT EXPERT

TIDE POOL TRIP

METEOR SLUMBER PARTY

CHALK ART MASTERPIECE

YOU'VE GOT TALENT

SHELLS ROCK!

LICENSE TO ADVENTURE

WHAT DOES AN OWL EAT?

STAND TALL ON HOMEMADE STILTS

FABULOUS FRUIT POPS

KAYAK TREK

SWEET SUMMER TREATS

"SUMMER AFTERNOON—
SUMMER AFTERNOON;
TO ME THOSE HAVE ALWAYS BEEN
THE TWO MOST BEAUTIFUL WORDS
IN THE ENGLISH LANGUAGE."
—HENRY JAMES

POET PRACTICE: SUMMER

BE A VOLUNTEER

MAKE A SUMMER NATURE COLLECTION

BACKPACKING FOR BEGINNERS

HAVE SOME MORE S'MORES

ECOSYSTEM EXPLORER

BECOME A BACKYARD NATURALIST

Naturalists study nature. They watch how nature changes due to seasons, weather, humans, and pollution. They get to know the behaviors of animals. They look at the health of plants and trees. They become experts on the nature around them.

You can be a naturalist too. All you need is a backyard or neighborhood park.

WHAT TO DO:

Observe

- Sit quietly outside and look for animals and birds that visit. Don't forget to watch for the animals that come at night.

- Turn over logs, lift rocks, and look on flowers to find insects.

- Notice the different plants.

Record

- Make a list of the birds, animals, insects, trees, flowers, and plants you find.

- Write a description and draw a picture or take a photo of each thing.

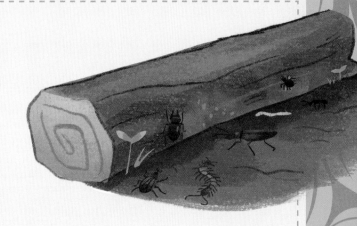

Learn

- Find out the names of each discovery with books, an app, or an internet search.

- Research if any of the plants are native to your area.

- Learn if the weeds in your area are invasive species.

Attract

- Learn what attracts other local animals, birds, or insects. Put those things in your yard.

  - Set up a light to attract moths and other insects.

  - Check your yard every week. Record any changes and new species.

- Keep watching for the whole summer and observe how things begin to change as autumn approaches.

MAKE A SUMMER NATURE COLLECTION

We spend a lot of time outdoors in the summer. That makes it easy to find all kinds of interesting things for a summer nature collection. Some of my family's favorite finds include seashells from the beach, like abalone, sand dollars, and urchin shells. We also have hawk and owl feathers, pine cones, and pieces of snakeskins. When we were camping in the Black Hills of South Dakota, we found pieces of mica and rose quartz right in our campsite! Looking at all these things reminds us of special summer moments.

We also save things we've found in our backyard or on walks in our neighborhood. We have a few tiny hummingbird nests. Did you know hummingbirds line their nests with soft things? Dryer lint or animal fur makes the nest soft and warm to protect the eggs. The nests we found in our backyard had lots of golden fur from our very hairy and fluffy dog, Shadow!

What special things can you add to your summer nature collection?

Tip: If you go on a summer trip, bring your collection notebook. Also bring a sturdy container to keep your items safe while you are traveling.

WHAT TO DO:

1. Decide on a place to keep your nature finds. You might use a shelf in your room. Or use a shelf in the living room if your parents say it's okay. You could also use a shoe box or a drawer in your dresser.
2. Find a small notebook to record your finds.
3. Look for special nature items every time you go outside. Make sure it's okay to take the items home.
4. In your notebook, identify what the item is, the date you found it, and where you found it. If you don't know what it is, do research to identify it. If your items are displayed on a shelf, you can make labels for each item with the same information.

It will be fun to look back at your summer nature collection. You'll remember your favorite summer adventures for the rest of the year.

June 21
Meadowlake Park
I found a bird's nest
made with leaves,
twigs, and moss.

SWEET SUMMER TREATS

Summer is the sweetest season! I love going to the farmers market or right into my backyard to get the most delicious fruit of the year. When I bite into a fresh peach, I am sure it's my favorite. But then I taste a ripe, purple plum, and I decide that one is my favorite! Then I try an apricot and, you guessed it, it's my new favorite. I guess it's too hard to choose.

I also love all the berries that are ripe in the summer. I think fresh strawberries have one of the best smells in the whole world. And there is nothing quite so delicious as eating a juicy blackberry right from the vine.

No matter what kind of fruit is your favorite, it's fun to find the freshest, ripest ones available and then turn them into a summer dessert. If you're like me and can't choose a favorite, you can mix them together. Or bake a few different fruit desserts over the summer.

First, discover which fruit grows where you live and when that fruit is ripe. Then find it at your local farmers market or visit a u-pick farm.

Find a recipe for the perfect fruit pie or crumble. Ask a parent, grandparent, other relative, or a friend if they have a recipe that they like. If they do, use that one. Or you can try my crumble recipe.

FRUIT CRUMBLE

What you need:

- **1 1/2 cups flour**
- **1/2 cup rolled oats**
- **1/3 cup brown sugar**
- **1/2 cup + 2 to 5 tablespoons white sugar**
- **1/4 teaspoon salt**
- **1 teaspoon cinnamon**
- **1/2 teaspoon ginger or allspice**
- **1/2 cup melted butter**
- **2 tablespoons cornstarch**
- **8 cups fresh fruit, cubed**
- **vanilla ice cream or whipped topping**

What to do:

1. Heat oven to 350 degrees.
2. To make the topping, mix the flour, oats, brown sugar, 1/2 cup white sugar, salt, cinnamon, and ginger (or allspice) in a large bowl. Stir in the melted butter until crumbs or little balls form.
3. To make the filling, mix remaining sugar and cornstarch in a separate large bowl. The amount of sugar will depend on the sweetness of the fruit. Then add the fruit. Gently coat the fruit with the sugar mixture.
4. Pour the fruit filling into a 10-inch cake pan. Spoon the topping over the filling.
5. Set the cake dish on top of a cookie sheet and put both into the oven. Bake until the filling is bubbling through the topping, about 50 minutes.
6. Let the crumble cool slightly. Serve with vanilla ice cream or whipped cream.

ADAPTED FROM COOKING.NYTIMES.COM.

BE A VOLUNTEER

Do you want to make a difference? Do you want to help people? One of the best ways to give to others is by volunteering your time.

And volunteering can be fun! It introduces us to new people and experiences. We see that the world is a lot bigger than our home, neighborhood, school, and church. There are people all over the world in need of help. You can help them!

Volunteering when you are a kid can sometimes be tricky though. At many organizations, you have to be over a certain age. Don't give up! Start by asking your parents to help you. They might need to volunteer with you. And then keep looking for a place to volunteer until you find the right one for you. You can make a difference in the world!

Tip: Volunteering is a great way to build friendships. Invite a couple buddies to serve with you and make a lasting memory!

WAYS KIDS CAN VOLUNTEER

- ☐ SELL BAKED GOODS, FRUIT PICKED FROM YOUR BACKYARD, OR HANDMADE ITEMS AND DONATE THE MONEY YOU MAKE TO SUPPORT AN ORGANIZATION YOU CARE ABOUT.
- ☐ WITH AN ADULT'S HELP, DELIVER MEALS TO ELDERLY PEOPLE.
- ☐ MAKE SMALL PACKETS OF HELPFUL ITEMS TO HAND OUT TO HOMELESS PEOPLE IN YOUR COMMUNITY. ASK A HOMELESS SHELTER WHAT ITEMS ARE BEST TO INCLUDE.
- ☐ HELP SCIENTISTS TRACK BIRDS BY TAKING PART IN THE GREAT BACKYARD BIRD COUNT.
- ☐ WRITE LETTERS AND CARDS TO SOLDIERS SERVING OVERSEAS.
- ☐ HELP A SICK, ELDERLY, OR WIDOWED NEIGHBOR BY TAKING OUT THEIR TRASH, PULLING WEEDS, RAKING LEAVES, OR SWEEPING THEIR SIDEWALK.
- ☐ PICK UP TRASH AT YOUR FAVORITE PARK, BEACH, RIVER, OR OTHER OUTDOOR SPOT.
- ☐ HAVE A BLANKET DRIVE FOR AN ANIMAL SHELTER IN YOUR COMMUNITY.
- ☐ ASK YOUR PASTOR WHO IN THE CONGREGATION NEEDS HELP. THEN MAKE A PLAN TO MEET THEIR NEEDS WITH YOUR FAMILY OR SUNDAY SCHOOL CLASS.
- ☐ JOIN A COMMUNITY DAY OF PLANTING TREES OR FLOWERS OR PULLING WEEDS.
- ☐ GATHER DONATIONS IN YOUR NEIGHBORHOOD FOR A CHARITY THRIFT STORE. SORT THROUGH THE ITEMS TO MAKE SURE THEY ARE IN GOOD CONDITION, AND THEN DELIVER THEM TO THE STORE.

TAKE A HIKE

My family loves to hike because we always make discoveries when we're on the trail. We've seen snakes, salamanders, and deer. Once we even saw a bear! We find wild plants that we can taste. We climb inside caves and to the top of tall rocks. Hiking out in nature is way more exciting than walking on a sidewalk!

FOLLOW THESE TIPS FOR YOUR BEST HIKING ADVENTURE:

- Hike in a new place.

- Look for butterflies, flowers, snakes, animals, birds, plants, and trees while you hike. When you find them, try to identify them with an app or a field guide.

- Bring your nature journal and stop to draw some of the things you see on your hike.

- Invite friends on a hike.

- Hike farther than you ever have before. Make a goal to complete a two-mile, five-mile, or even ten-mile hike within a year's time. Increase your distance a little bit on each hike until you reach your goal.

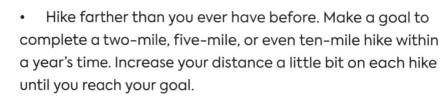

THE TEN ESSENTIALS FOR HIKING

1. **Backpack:** You'll want a comfortable backpack to carry your supplies.
2. **Water:** One medium or large water bottle. Bring an extra if it is a warm day.
3. **Snacks:** Pack lots of snacks. Some good ideas are jerky, trail mix, fruit, granola bars, or peanut butter and crackers. Ask if you can pack a special treat, like a small chocolate bar, dried fruit, or a cookie for an extra push on the hardest parts of the trail.
4. **Towel:** A small, lightweight towel gives you a place to sit and eat your snacks. You can also use it if you get wet.
5. **Toilet paper and baggies:** You never know if you'll have to go to the bathroom on a hike.
6. **First aid kit:** Include a pair of tweezers, Band-Aids of all sizes, antibiotic cream, alcohol wipes, and bug spray. Ask an adult if you should include allergy medicine and pain relievers.
7. **Sun protection:** Bring a hat and sunscreen. Use them even on cloudy days. You can still get a sunburn through clouds.
8. **Layered clothing:** You never know when the weather will turn hot or cold, so be ready.
9. **Preparation:** The night before, pack your backpack. Fill water bottles, get the snacks ready, and use this checklist to make sure you have all your gear.
10. **A positive attitude:** Having a cheerful heart will make the adventure so much better!

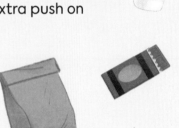

FIRST AID

STAND TALL ON HOMEMADE STILTS

When I was a girl, I read a book in which the character made stilts out of tin cans. Maybe you have read it too. It's called *Ramona the Brave.* I decided I wanted to make tin-can stilts just like Ramona did. They weren't hard to make, and I had so much fun clomping down the sidewalk on my homemade stilts.

When my kids read that same book, they also wanted to make tin-can stilts. You can too!

WHAT YOU NEED:

two empty tin cans
> For taller stilts, use coffee cans.
> For medium stilts, use 29-ounce cans.
> For short stilts, use tuna cans.

wrapping paper or fabric and clear craft glue (optional)

four medium-sized nails

thin rope or twine

flexible tape measure

hammer

WHAT TO DO:

1. Wash the cans. Peel labels off the cans and let them dry.
2. If you'd like to decorate your stilts, use wrapping paper or fabric. With a flexible tape measure, measure around a can to determine the length of the fabric. Measure the height of the can for the width of the fabric. Measure the paper or fabric and cut out two strips. Brush craft glue over the sides of one can and wrap the paper or fabric around it. Press into the glue. Then brush another layer of glue over the top of the paper or fabric. Repeat with the second can. Let dry overnight.
3. Mark a spot about one inch from the bottom of the can. On the exact opposite side of the can, make another mark.
4. With a hammer, tap a nail into each spot.
5. Repeat marking and nailing with the second can.
6. Measure how long to make the rope handles. Stick one end of the rope or twine through one hole into the can. Then thread it through the can and out the other hole. Stand on the can and pull the end of the rope up until it sits comfortably in your hand when you stand straight. Bring the other end of the rope up until the rope is the same length on each side. Take a step. Adjust the rope length if you need more room to stand up all the way or if you need the rope tighter to easily pull the can up.

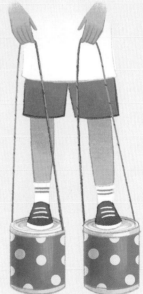

7. Cut the rope to the correct length and tie the ends together in a tight knot.
8. Cut another piece of rope or twine the same length as the first piece, thread it through the other can, and tie the ends together.
9. Step into your stilts and practice with slow steps. Keep practicing. Before you know it, you'll be clomping down the sidewalk on your stilts!

METEOR SLUMBER PARTY

Every summer from mid-July to mid-August, a beautiful meteor shower lights up the night sky. The meteors come from the area near the constellation named for Perseus, the hero of Greek myths, so it's called the Perseids (say *Per-see-ids*) meteor shower.

Every year at this time, our earth crosses the path of a comet called Swift-Tuttle. The comet carries bits of dust and rock that crash into our atmosphere at superfast speeds, which makes them light up. These are meteors.

It's incredibly exciting to see these beautiful meteors streak across the sky. And you never know when the next one is coming! It's a peek at the magic that happens in the vast expanse of space that's usually too far away to see.

Don't miss the next Perseids meteor shower!

WHAT TO DO:

Plan the best time to see the meteor shower.

1. Research the nights when astronomers predict the meteor shower will peak. This is usually two to three nights in early August.
2. Check the forecast for clouds or fog that will make it difficult to see the sky.
3. Make plans to see the meteors on a peak night that is clear.
4. If you are going to stay up late to see the showers, take a nap that day. If you are going to wake up before dawn, go to bed early.

Get ready to see some meteors.

1. Travel to a place in the country away from lights where you have a wide-open view of the sky.
2. Let your eyes adjust to the darkness for about twenty minutes. Don't use a flashlight or a cell phone during this time or your eyes will have to start all over again.
3. Give yourself at least an hour to see a meteor. The showers come in bursts, so it might be a while before you see one. Be patient.
4. Sit back and enjoy the beautiful fireworks display that God made for you.
5. When it's time to go, ask an adult to stop for donuts on the way home!

Pack supplies you'll need while you watch.

- blanket or a lawn chair that reclines

- extra blankets to cover up with

- hot chocolate or other drink to sip while you wait

ALL TIED UP

Tying knots is a good camping and outdoor skill. If you go backpacking, you will want to tie your food up in a tree where animals can't get to it. You'll also want to know how to tie down a tent or tarp securely in windy and wet conditions. You need knot-tying skills to fasten a kayak to a car or tie up a boat at a dock. If you are rock climbing, a strong, secure knot can save your life.

Tying knots also helps your brain get stronger. It's a kind of riddle or puzzle to solve. It's also great exercise for your memory. You have to remember all the steps it takes to tie each kind of knot.

A great knot to start with is the square knot. You probably already know how to start this knot. You make the first half of a square knot when you tie your shoes.

KNOTS TO LEARN

☐ CLOVE HITCH
☐ BOWLINE
☐ FIGURE-EIGHT LOOP
☐ TAUT-LINE HITCH
☐ SLIPKNOT
☐ SHEET BEND
☐ HARNESS HITCH
☐ CARRICK BEND
☐ BARREL HITCH

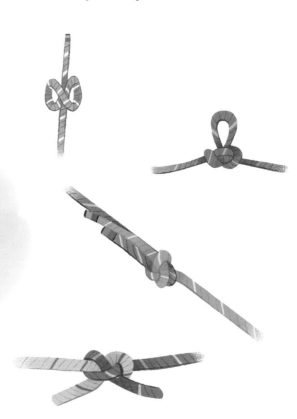

HOW TO TIE A SQUARE KNOT

WHAT YOU NEED: paracord or nylon rope

WHAT TO DO:

1. Hold an end of the rope in each hand.

2. Pass the right end over and under the rope in your left hand.

3. Pass the rope end now in your left hand over and under the one now in your right.

4. Tighten the knot by pulling both running ends at the same time.

There are lots of different knots to learn. Watch videos and keep practicing, and you'll be ready to tie up any situation.

HAVE SOME MORE S'MORES

One day I was at the market shopping for a camping trip. I knew I needed to get supplies for my kids to make s'mores. *I wish I liked eating s'mores*, I thought as I gathered marshmallows and graham crackers.

Then a new idea struck me. What if I changed out some of the s'mores ingredients to ones I liked better? So I filled my cart with different ingredients.

A few days later, we sat around the campfire, and I pulled out everything to make s'mores. "What are these things?" my family asked, pointing to the new ingredients.

"I thought we could try making s'mores with new things," I said. They were so excited and immediately started brainstorming new s'mores combinations. We spent the whole summer trying the different recipes.

Do some creative cooking and have a s'mores-making competition!

WHAT TO DO:

1. Invite your friends to the competition. Ask each one to come up with a new recipe for s'mores and bring the ingredients with them.
2. With an adult's help, build a campfire in a safe place.
3. Have each person make their own version of s'mores.
4. Give each s'mores sample to adult judges to taste and choose a winner.
5. Ask each person to share the ingredients they chose for their s'mores.
6. Sample one or two of the new s'mores created by your friends.

Here's my recipe for s'mores. I hope you try them.

S'MORES

What you need:

thin butter waffle cookies
chocolate hazelnut spread
jumbo marshmallows

What to do:

1. Spread a thin layer of chocolate hazelnut spread on two cookies.
2. Toast your marshmallow until golden brown on each side. Do not allow it to burn.
3. Sandwich the marshmallow between the two cookies and slide the marshmallow off the roasting stick.
4. Eat and enjoy!

THE PERFECT PET

When I was a girl, I longed for a pet of my own. But my little brother was allergic to any animal with fur. So there weren't many pets I could have. I tried fish, but they weren't cuddly. Next, I got a hermit crab. He was cute, but his little aquarium got stinky if I didn't clean it often. I wanted a pet that was cute, cuddly, and easy.

That's when I heard about pet rocks. A pet rock wasn't cuddly, but it could be cute. And once I painted it, it was no work at all! A pet rock was the pet for me.

WHAT YOU NEED:

- **smooth rocks collected from outside or bought from a store**
- **acrylic paints**
- **newspaper, paper grocery bags, or an old sheet to paint on**
- **an old T-shirt, smock, or apron you can get messy**
- **paintbrushes of various sizes**
- **paint pens (optional; to make more intricate designs or write words)**

WHAT TO DO:

You can have any pet rock you can imagine. Here are a few fun options:

- Paint a dog, a cat, a lion, or even a dinosaur.
- Make a pet family or a whole zoo to line up on a shelf in your room.
- Create a rock garden by drawing flowers, a sun, or leaves on your rocks.
- Design your rock with intricate intersecting lines or other shapes.
- Paint encouraging words on rocks. Leave them out for people to find. Place them in your front yard, at a playground, or near a path where people ride bikes or jog.
- Be sure to let your new pet dry completely before cuddling!

KAYAK TREK

Going kayaking is a new way to experience the water. My favorite place to go kayaking is in Morro Bay, California. When we kayak there, we see seals, sea otters, all kinds of fish, stingrays, and pelicans, as well as many other birds.

No matter where you live, you can find a lake, river, bay, or ocean and have your own kayaking adventure.

WHAT YOU NEED:

- kayaks and paddles
- drinking water and food
- life jackets
- sun protection
- a waterproof bag for your camera, food, and dry clothes
- waterproof shoes or shoes that can get wet
- a rope to tie up the kayak on breaks
- first aid kit

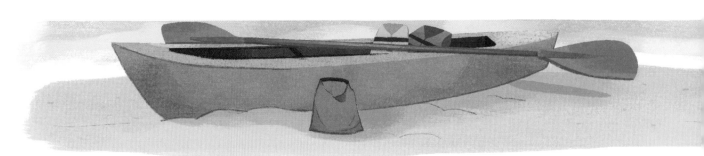

REMEMBER SAFETY MEASURES:

- Always wear a life jacket.

- Don't go out alone.

- If you are new to kayaking, get instructions before you get out on the water. Learn how to steer the boat, get in and out of the boat, and fall out and get back in if the boat flips.

- Wear a helmet if paddling in rough water.

- Check the weather before you go.

DIFFERENT WAYS TO EXPLORE THE WATER:

- ☐ TAKE A SAILING CLASS.
- ☐ TRY PADDLEBOARDING IN A CALM BODY OF WATER. YOU CAN SHARE A RENTAL WITH A FEW FRIENDS AND TAKE TURNS USING IT TOGETHER.
- ☐ FIND A RIVER WITH CLASS 1 RAPIDS, JOIN A GROUP WITH A GUIDE, AND TRY RIVER RAFTING!
- ☐ CANOE IN A CALM RIVER, LAKE, BAYOU, OR BAY.
- ☐ FIND AN ADULT WITH A FISHING BOAT AND ASK TO GO ON THEIR NEXT FISHING TRIP.

July 3

Morro Bay

On our kayaking adventure today, we went right by this old ship!

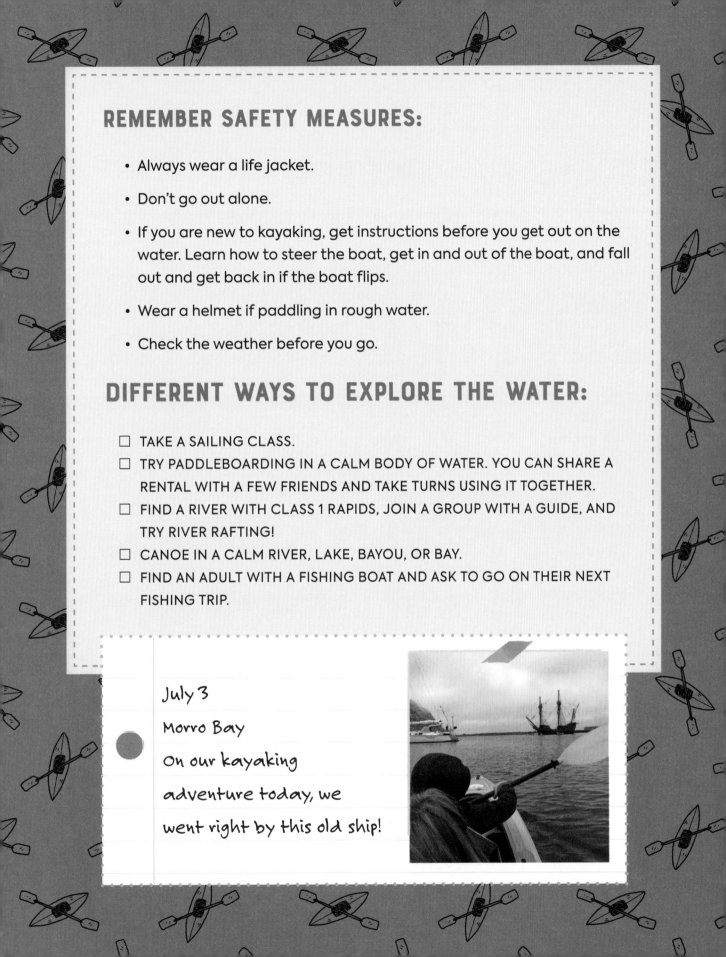

ECOSYSTEM EXPLORER

I love to explore new spots out in nature. I like to see the different plants, animals, trees, and birds that I don't see at home. I remember the first time I saw a beautiful bright red cardinal when I was hiking in Tennessee. We don't have cardinals where I live in California, so I was very, very excited when his bright red feathers told me who he was. This is the fun of exploring new eco-systems. You are sure to make discoveries.

WHAT TO DO:

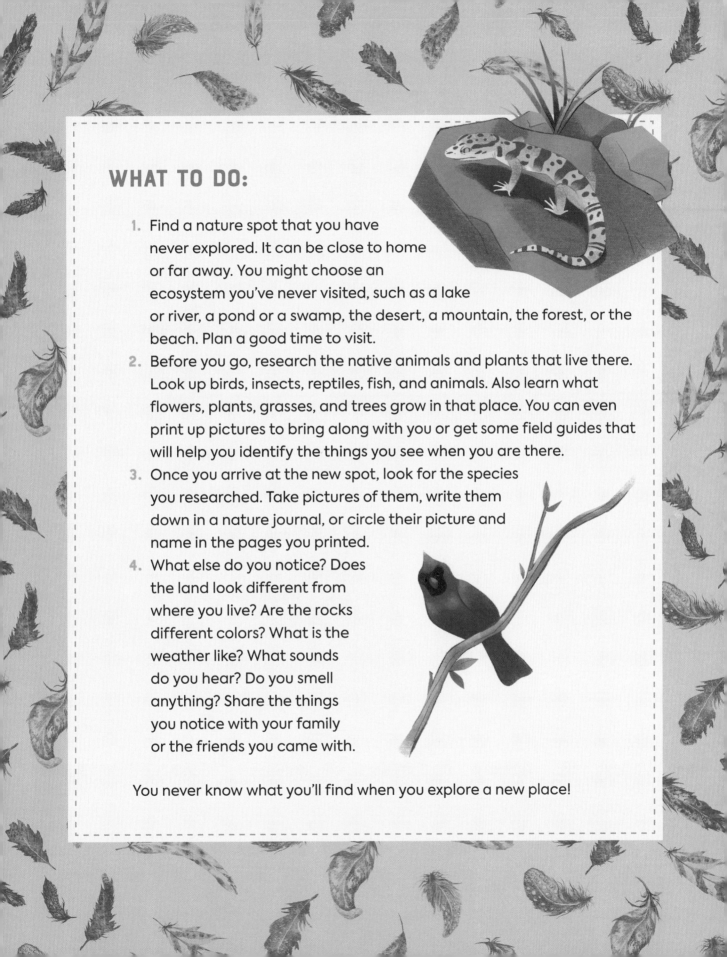

1. Find a nature spot that you have never explored. It can be close to home or far away. You might choose an ecosystem you've never visited, such as a lake or river, a pond or a swamp, the desert, a mountain, the forest, or the beach. Plan a good time to visit.

2. Before you go, research the native animals and plants that live there. Look up birds, insects, reptiles, fish, and animals. Also learn what flowers, plants, grasses, and trees grow in that place. You can even print up pictures to bring along with you or get some field guides that will help you identify the things you see when you are there.

3. Once you arrive at the new spot, look for the species you researched. Take pictures of them, write them down in a nature journal, or circle their picture and name in the pages you printed.

4. What else do you notice? Does the land look different from where you live? Are the rocks different colors? What is the weather like? What sounds do you hear? Do you smell anything? Share the things you notice with your family or the friends you came with.

You never know what you'll find when you explore a new place!

SHELLS ROCK!

When I was a girl, I loved collecting shells so much that I started a seashell club with my friends. We collected shells whenever we went to the beach. We also asked grandparents, aunts, uncles, and friends to bring back shells when they traveled. We tried to learn the names of our shells and what sea creatures once lived in them. When we saw each other for playdates, we brought our shells and traded them with one another. I loved my seashell club.

I enjoyed collecting rocks too. Rocks were easier to find than shells because I could dig them up from the tall, rocky bank that formed part of our backyard. I found all kinds of quartz and granite rocks there. And it seemed like every time we went into a campground gift store or to the mall, there were bins of beautiful, smooth, colored rocks. I saved my money to buy different kinds of rocks and kept everything in a neat little case.

Do you love collecting shells or rocks? Start a club with your friends!

WHAT TO DO:

1. Think of some friends who like collecting nature things. Invite them to be in your club.
2. Schedule your first meeting. Tell your friends to bring their shell, rock, or other kind of nature collection. Let them know that if they want to trade items with other people in the club they can.
3. Choose a place to host the meeting. Good places might be your backyard, kitchen, or the park.
4. Set up a table or spread blankets on the ground for everyone to lay out their collections.
5. When your club members arrive, ask them to set out their collections. Then look around at all the items. Ask questions about your friends' collections. What is their favorite piece? Where did the piece come from?
6. After everyone has looked at the collections, give time to trade for anyone who wants to.
7. Make plans for your next meeting. Wait a few months, until you've all had time to get new shells or rocks.

LICENSE TO ADVENTURE

I still remember my very first library card. It was made of thick, cream-colored paper and had a drawing of books on it. There was a line at the bottom where I signed my name very neatly with my favorite pen. After the librarian checked my signature, she handed the card back to me. "Congratulations," she said, "now you can check out your very own books!" I carefully placed the library card in my wallet. Then I went off to my favorite section of the library to check out as many books as they would let me bring home. All on my very own library card!

WHAT TO DO:

1. Ask an adult to help you look up exactly what you need to get a library card from the library in your town.
2. Fill out a library card application. Sometimes you can print out the application from the library's website and fill it out at home. Or you can just get the application at the library. Try to fill it out all by yourself if you can. But if you get stuck, an adult can help you.
3. At the library, go to the front desk and turn in your form. The librarian will give you your own card to sign. Write your name on it neatly.
4. Put your card in a safe place so you do not lose it.
5. Go check out some books and begin a new adventure!

POET PRACTICE: SUMMER

Did you know that poetry existed before people even wrote things down? In ancient days, people shared poems and important stories of their culture, religion, and history out loud. They also used poetry to teach young people how to do things. And sometimes they just shared poems aloud for fun. You can learn poems for fun too. Try learning a poem for the summer season, and then share it out loud with someone.

Sea Shell

Sea Shell, Sea Shell,
Sing me a song, O Please!
A song of ships, and sailor men,
And parrots, and tropical trees,
Of islands lost in the
    Spanish Main,
Which no man ever may find
    again,
Of fishes and corals under the
    waves,
And seahorses stabled in great
    green caves.
Sea Shell, Sea Shell,
Sing of the things you know
    so well.
    —Amy Lowell
from *A Dome of Many-
Colored Glass*, 1912

SUMMER POEMS

Here are some other poems that celebrate summer. Look them up and read them aloud.

**"Summer in the South" by
Paul Laurence Dunbar
"Firefly" by Jacqueline
Woodson
"June" by John Updike
"Here Comes" by
Shel Silverstein**

INSECT EXPERT

Do you know what insects live in your yard? You've probably seen ants, snails, and maybe a spider or some bees. But do you know the name of the spider you saw? Or the type of bee you saw? Did you know there are twenty thousand different kinds of bees? Wow!

And I bet if you look hard enough around your yard, you might even find some insects that you've never seen before. Some of the most interesting insects we've found in our yard are a green lynx spider, a swallowtail butterfly, a Jerusalem cricket, and my most favorite, a katydid. When I was a girl, we used to have big, hairy tarantulas that walked through our yard at the end of every summer.

Imagine what kinds of cool insects are hiding all over your backyard! Now head outside and find some.

WHAT TO DO:

1. Turn over rocks, look under leaves or mulch, and roll over logs. Look on the leaves of plants and trees. Dig up some dirt.
2. When you find an insect, make sure it's not an insect that will harm you. Then gently capture it.
3. Put it in a clear container with holes in the top so the insect can breathe.
4. Research the insect's name and learn about its habits and what it eats.
5. If you can find the right food for it, put some in with the insect. Provide water too.
6. Observe your insect for a day.
7. Set the insect free where you found it.
8. Look for a new one tomorrow!

July 16
Prairie Creek
Redwoods State Park
This bright green
polyphemus caterpillar
wrapped himself
around a twig like a
monkey's tail.

ON THE ROAD

I love road trips! There is something new to see at every mile.

I remember taking road trips with my mom and dad when I was younger. Often my dad would travel for work, and in summertime we could go with him. Once we drove hours and hours to a coastal town in California. It was thrilling to eat clam chowder at a restaurant right over the water where we could watch seals playing below us.

Another time we drove just two hours to the mountains where I got to try horseback riding on a trail for the first time. It was scary *and* fun!

What kind of road trip adventure can you plan for your family? Here are some ideas to get you started dreaming.

- Drive down a famous highway. You might choose the Pacific Coast Highway in California, Route 66 through the deserts of New Mexico and Arizona, the Going-to-the-Sun Road in Glacier National Park, the Blue Ridge Parkway in North Carolina and Virginia, or many others.

- Try out river rafting. Some famous places are the Gauley River in West Virginia, the Colorado River in Arizona, the Salmon River in Idaho, and the Kennebec River in Maine.

- Read a book and take a road trip to where the book takes place. Read *Misty of Chincoteague* by Marguerite Henry, then drive out to see the wild horses on Assateague Island, Virginia. Read *The Watsons Go to Birmingham* and visit some of the Watsons' stopping points as they traveled from Michigan to Alabama. Read the Little House books by Laura Ingalls Wilder and visit the Ingalls homestead in South Dakota. Read the Ramona Quimby books by Beverly Cleary and visit spots from the books in Portland, Oregon. Read *Children of the Longhouse* by Joseph Bruchac and visit the part of upstate New York where the Mohawk tribe lived.

- Travel to a beach, lake, or river where you can collect shells, rocks, or sea glass.

- Explore a big city like Chicago, New York, or Seattle.

- Find a state or national park near you full of great hikes.

Tip: On any kind of adventure, things don't always go according to plan. When that happens, our family prays together for things to get better. We also pray that we will all have good attitudes until they do. And do you know what? Those bumps in the road always make the best stories later!

WHAT DOES AN OWL EAT?

I used to see these strange things under trees in my neighborhood that looked like gray, furry poop. I always wondered what they were. Later, I learned they came from owls. But they aren't owl poop. They're called owl pellets. And owls actually throw them up.

So gross, right? Actually though, they aren't that icky. They don't smell bad. And the fact is owls have to throw up those pellets to survive! You see, an owl eats small rodents, reptiles, and other birds. But it can't digest the bones, scales, fur, and feathers of those animals. So a part of the owl's stomach, called the gizzard, squishes all those things into a ball. Then the owl throws up the pellet and is ready to eat another meal.

Once I learned all about owl pellets, I wanted to dissect one and see what was inside. My family had seen owls up in a tree in a park near our house, so we gathered pellets from under the tree.

We took our owl pellets home and carefully dissected them. We found many small bones and even a couple full skulls! I love exploring. Even if I'm exploring owl barf.

What will you find in your own owl pellet?

Tip: To find an owl pellet in nature, look for white droppings all over the ground under trees. That means owls like to roost and nest there.

WHAT YOU NEED:

- disposable gloves
- owl pellet
- newspaper or paper bags to work on
- two twigs or popsicle sticks
- tweezers
- clean sheet of paper
- printout of the animal bones commonly found in owl pellets

WHAT TO DO:

1. Find an owl pellet in nature or order one from a nature store. If you find a pellet in nature, use disposable gloves to pick it up and store it in a disposable plastic bag or container.

2. Spread the newspaper or paper bags on a table and put on your gloves.

3. Carefully pull apart the owl pellet with your fingers or the sticks.

4. Use tweezers to pull out the tiny bones. Set them on the sheet of paper.

5. Try to identify the different kinds of animal bones with your identification chart.

6. After you are done investigating the owl pellet, place all the pieces of the pellet, the bones, and all other disposable materials in the trash. Wipe down the work area with soapy water and disposable towels. Also, wash the tweezers.

7. If you'd like to keep the animal bones you found in the owl pellet, leave them outside in the sun for a few days to kill any germs.

YOU'VE GOT TALENT!

Talent shows are a lot of fun, no matter which side of the stage you are on. It's inspiring to see all the different things people can do. Host a talent show in your own backyard on a summer night, when the air is warm and the sun sets late.

TALENT IDEAS

Tell jokes.

Do magic tricks.

Share a piece of art.

Perform a skit.

Do a dance.

Do tricks with a pet.

Recite a famous speech or poem.

Sing.

Share homemade food.

Play an instrument.

Juggle.

Do tricks with a yo-yo.

Perform gymnastics.

Lip-sync to a song.

Do jump rope tricks.

Dribble a soccer or basketball.

Do impressions.

Tell a story.

Hula-Hoop.

Perform a puppet show.

Perform card tricks.

Show a decorated cake.

Whistle a song.

Share a Lego build.

Create balloon animals.

WHAT TO DO:

Plan

- Decide when to hold the show.

- About a month before, send invitations to everyone who will be in the talent show and in the audience. You can handwrite the invitations, send an email, or ask a grown-up to let you call or text people. Include a deadline in the invitation for people to sign up to perform and let you know their talent. Make the deadline at least a week before the show.

Prepare

- Practice the talent you'll be sharing in the talent show.

- Prepare a program with the names and talents of the people performing. Print the program to hand out to guests.

- Plan your stage. It can be a raised area of your yard like a deck or patio. It can also just be an area of your yard where the performers will stand, with blankets or chairs around it for the audience.

- Decide whether to provide snacks, and plan, shop for, and make them.

- Pick an emcee to announce the performers. The emcee will read the names from the program.

Perform

- On the night of the show, thank everyone for coming and for sharing their talents.

- Let the show begin!

FABULOUS FRUIT POPS

Popsicles are a great part of summer, aren't they? On a hot day, it's so refreshing to pull a popsicle out of the freezer and let its sweet, cool juice fill your belly.

My family likes to make homemade popsicles, using whatever ripe fruit or juice we have on hand. Sometimes we squeeze lemons, mix the juice with crushed-up strawberries, and make strawberry lemonade popsicles. Other times we put chunks of watermelon in the blender, whir it up, and make watermelon popsicles. We also turn fruit smoothies into popsicles and eat them for breakfast!

Tip: To remove popsicles from molds, run under warm water for a few seconds.

FRUIT SMOOTHIE POPSICLES

What you need:

- **6 cups fresh fruit, chopped**
- **2 tablespoons honey or white sugar**
- **2/3 cup vanilla Greek yogurt**
- **10 popsicle molds**

What to do:

1. Blend the fruit and honey or sugar in a blender until smooth.
2. Spoon 2 teaspoons of fruit into each popsicle mold. Add 1 teaspoon yogurt. Repeat until the mold is filled. End with a fruit layer.
3. Tap the mold gently on the counter to make the layers settle. Freeze for at least 6 hours.

ADAPTED FROM WWW.JESSICAGAVIN.COM.

FABULOUS FRUIT FLAVORS

strawberry peach
banana mango pineapple
orange raspberry banana
berry banana
orange pineapple

kiwi strawberry
cherry banana
blueberry pear
pineapple coconut

CHALK ART MASTERPIECE

One of the best ways to be a better artist is to study the works of famous masters and re-create them yourself. Artists have been using this study method for hundreds and hundreds of years.

But instead of drawing out your favorite artwork with pencil and paper, try using bold, bright chalk. Your driveway or sidewalk will be your canvas. Working in a large space gives you lots of room to create and interpret the drawing to make it your own.

You can choose a painting by a modern artist with big blocks of color. Or find an artist who drew simple things found around the house, like bouquets of flowers or bowls of fruit. If you're especially ambitious, try a landscape scene. You'll have fun comparing your own work with the piece of art that inspired it.

WHAT TO DO:

1. Browse art books or the internet to find a painting or drawing that inspires you.
2. Look closely at the piece of art. What does the artist focus on? What kinds of shapes and lines do they use—sharp edges, smooth curves, bold outlines? How do they use light and shadow? How does the artwork make you feel?
3. Look at the colors the artist used. Gather chalks in similar colors.
4. If you want a practice run, make a simple sketch of the drawing. It doesn't have to be an exact copy. It should be your own version.
5. Find a shady spot to work in or put on a sun hat. Don't forget the sunscreen!
6. Get to work on creating your masterpiece. From time to time, get up and step back to check your work and look again at your sketch or a picture of the original piece.

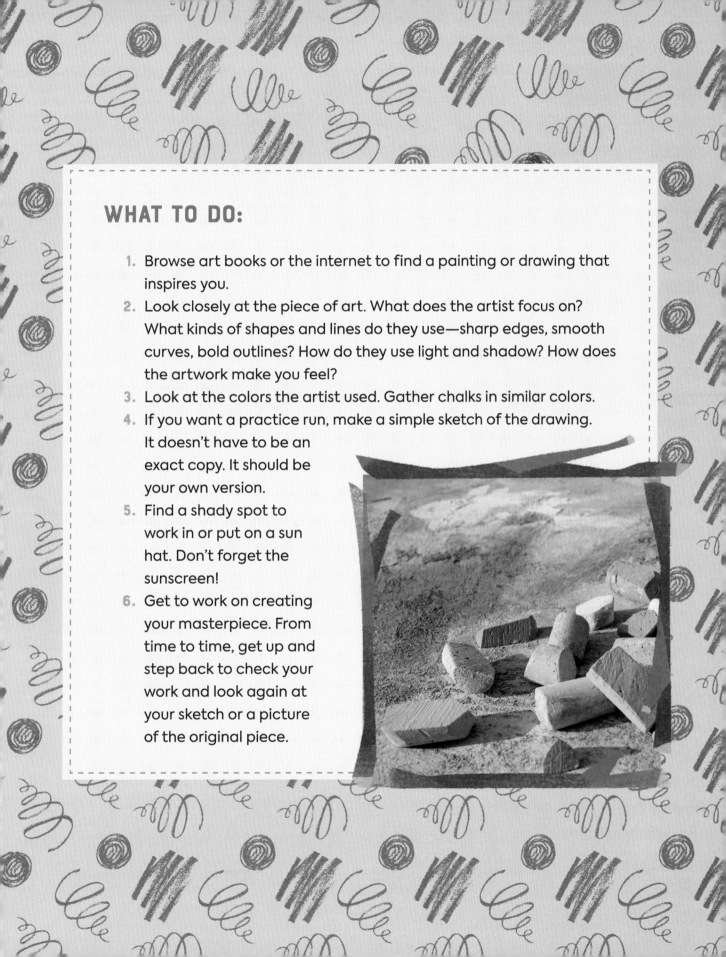

BACKPACKING FOR BEGINNERS

When I was young, my dad told me stories of his backpacking trip in the mountains of Yosemite National Park. He and his friends hiked so far into the wilderness that all they saw on the trail were wild animals like deer and bears. They swam in perfectly clear, icy cold alpine lakes and drank from streams. They cooked food on tiny backpacking stoves and slept in warm sleeping bags under the stars.

I wanted more than anything to go on a backpacking trip just like my dad did. But I had to wait a long time. I didn't go on that backpacking trip until I was a grown-up. When I did, I took my kids along. Some parts of our trip were hard, but after we hiked back down to the car, everyone said they wanted to do another backpacking trip as soon as we could!

You can go on a backpack-ing adventure too.

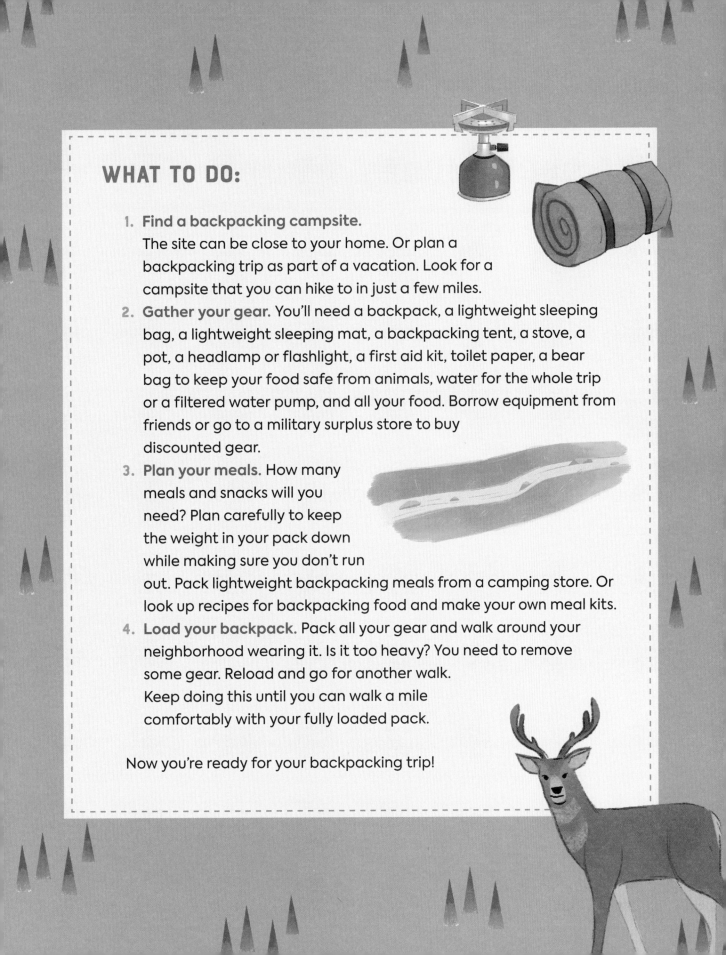

WHAT TO DO:

1. **Find a backpacking campsite.**
   The site can be close to your home. Or plan a backpacking trip as part of a vacation. Look for a campsite that you can hike to in just a few miles.

2. **Gather your gear.** You'll need a backpack, a lightweight sleeping bag, a lightweight sleeping mat, a backpacking tent, a stove, a pot, a headlamp or flashlight, a first aid kit, toilet paper, a bear bag to keep your food safe from animals, water for the whole trip or a filtered water pump, and all your food. Borrow equipment from friends or go to a military surplus store to buy discounted gear.

3. **Plan your meals.** How many meals and snacks will you need? Plan carefully to keep the weight in your pack down while making sure you don't run out. Pack lightweight backpacking meals from a camping store. Or look up recipes for backpacking food and make your own meal kits.

4. **Load your backpack.** Pack all your gear and walk around your neighborhood wearing it. Is it too heavy? You need to remove some gear. Reload and go for another walk. Keep doing this until you can walk a mile comfortably with your fully loaded pack.

Now you're ready for your backpacking trip!

THE SHOW MUST GO OUT

Most people think of being inside when they think of seeing a play or hearing a concert. But during the summertime, musical and theater groups move outdoors. In Los Angeles's outdoor theater called the Hollywood Bowl, concertgoers can enjoy everything from rock shows to film concerts where a live orchestra plays the songs from movies like *Star Wars* and *The Sound of Music*. In Ashland, Oregon, you can watch a Shakespeare play in an outdoor theater that's built to look like a theater from Shakespeare's day. And near Denver, Colorado, you can listen to a concert in an amphitheater built right into giant red rocks.

But you don't have to go to a big venue to see a great performance. All over, county fairs host bands, dance groups, magicians, and animal shows. Community theater groups perform Shakespeare in the park. Music groups perform in downtown squares on cool summer nights. I bet there are some neat summer performances where you live too!

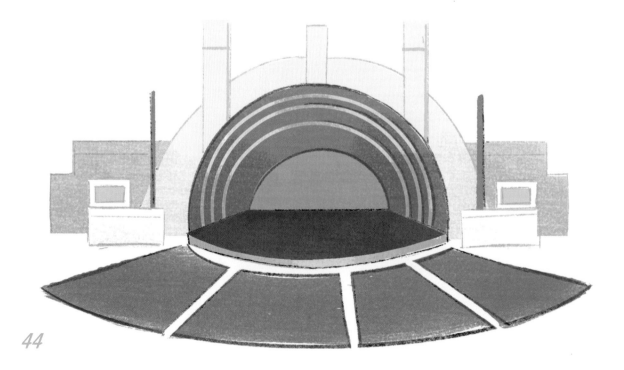

WHAT TO DO:

1. Think about the kind of outdoor performance you want to see. Is it a famous music star? You'll want to find a concert or music festival. Is it an orchestra? Most cities have symphonies with outdoor dates. Is it a play? Community theaters often have outdoor performances. Is it a dance performance? You'll be looking for a ballet company, cultural festival, or holiday celebration.
2. Research with an adult to find an event near you this summer.
3. When you go to the event, bring a blanket or folding chair to sit on. If it gets chilly at night where you live, bring a sweater or jacket. Pack food and drinks for a picnic. Or, if the venue doesn't allow outside food, bring money to buy food from the concession stands or food trucks.

TIDE POOL TRIP

One of my favorite activities at the beach is tide pooling. When the tide comes in, seawater fills pools created by rocks. The animals living in the pools come out from under the rocks or plants. They feast on the plankton that float in with the water. When the tide goes back out, the animals return to their rock or plant homes to take shelter from the hot sun.

August 2

Point Loma Tide Pools

Giant Spined Sea Star

Tip: If you can't visit a tide pool, you can make one! Research "tide pool animals" on the internet or in books, then make a tide pool diorama in a shoe box. Glue in real sand and rocks. Use blue tissue paper or plastic cellophane sheets to make water. Then create tide pool animals by printing out photos, drawing them, or molding clay. Share your diorama with someone and tell them about the tide pool animals.

BEFORE YOU GO:

1. Find a tide pool area to visit. Do a web search for "tide pool" plus the name of a city or beach near you or where you'll be traveling.
2. Plan to visit the tide pools at low tide. You can find out the time of low tide by doing a web search for your beach's name plus "tide times."
3. Look up the tide pool creatures that live in your tide pool area, so you'll recognize them when you see them.

WHAT TO BRING:

water shoes or sneakers that you can get wet

sunscreen and a hat

drinking water

towel

clear plastic bowls or containers

tide pool animal identification guide (optional)

WHAT TO DO:

1. Walk carefully onto the rocks of the tide pools. They are often slippery and sharp.
2. Squat down to look into pools and peer under rocks or through plants.
3. Spend a little time in one place waiting to see what animals swim or crawl by. If you are patient, you will be rewarded.
4. Carefully catch fish, crabs, sea urchins, or sea slugs in your container. Observe them for a few minutes, then release them back to the pool. Don't try to pry an animal off a rock if it is firmly attached. Just observe it where it is.
5. When the tide begins to come in, leave the tide pools to stay safe from the incoming waves.

NATURE'S SWIMMING POOLS

Have you ever swum in a swimming hole? My favorite swimming hole has deep water surrounded by big rocks. The first time I jumped in, I held my nose and screamed the whole way down. Everyone laughed.

I especially like swimming holes that are fed by waterfalls. The falls send their cold, clear water cascading down. Hot summer days are the best time to visit a swimming hole because after a sweaty hike, there is nothing so refreshing as jumping into that cold water.

WHAT TO DO:

1. Find a swimming hole near you. Look for a deep spot at the base of a waterfall, a wide spot in a creek, or a shallow spot in a river.
2. If you must hike to get to your swimming hole, pack water, snacks, sun protection, and a towel.
3. Before you get in the swimming hole, ask an adult to help you look for fast currents or rocks or branches underwater that could hurt you.
4. Once the adult says it is safe to get in, make a splash!

FALL ACTIVITIES

TAKE A RIDE

CONDUCT YOURSELF TO A SYMPHONY CONCERT

MAKE A FALL NATURE COLLECTION

GARDEN IN A JAR

ROCKS, GEMS, AND MINERALS, OH MY!

KNEAD TO BAKE BREAD

BUILD AN OUTDOOR FORT

"I'M SO GLAD I LIVE IN A WORLD WHERE THERE ARE OCTOBERS."

– L.M. MONTGOMERY, ANNE OF GREEN GABLES

DARE TO TRY

CLIMB TO NEW HEIGHTS

MAKE WAXED LEAVES

DEEP SEA SIGHTSEEING

A FAIRLY CRAFTY AFFAIR

WRITE TO A SOLDIER

PLAN A BOOK CLUB

POET PRACTICE: FALL

RAINY-DAY RAMBLE

CREATE A COLLECTION

DISCOVER NATIONAL TREASURES

HAWK-EYED HOBBY

THE TASTE OF FALL

TAKE A (FOREST) BATH

CHALK UP A SMILE

LEARN TO HAND STITCH

PICK AND DRY APPLES

GET FIRED UP

TAKE A (FOREST) BATH

Have you ever heard of forest bathing? Forest bathing comes from Japan. The idea is to soak in the peace and happiness of the woods.

Science tells us that spending time in nature is good for our health. Time outdoors strengthens our immune system, so we get sick less often. It helps us worry less, and it puts us in a good mood.

Forests seem to give us an extra dose of peace. The trees are tall and strong. They provide us with shelter and protection from the sun and wind and rain. In the forest, leaves blanket the ground and soften the sounds of the world. Even the way the trees smell can make us feel better. The forest is a wonderful place to find calm. John Muir, one of America's most well-known naturalists, said, "Come to the woods, for here is rest."

Find a nearby forest to visit, and bathe in the fresh air, soft sounds, and quiet calm.

WHAT TO BRING:

blanket or towel
water
snack
nature journal

WHAT TO DO:

1. Follow a trail that will take you into the woods.
2. Find a quiet place to sit away from people. Try to get a little way off the main path.
3. Spread your blanket and sit still. Breathe in the peace of the forest.
4. Concentrate on the sounds, smells, sights, and textures all around you. What do you hear? What do you smell? What do you see? What can you touch?
5. Make notes about what you notice in your nature journal. Draw a picture of the trees. Or write a poem about what you hear, smell, see, and touch.
6. Visit the forest again soon for another bath in the calm of the woods.

MAKE WAXED LEAVES

One of my favorite parts of fall is the way the leaves change color. But I don't like how fast the leaves fall off the trees and turn into a big, brown mess in the yard. I want to see their bright colors for much longer! So one year, I decided to preserve the leaves in wax and keep their bright beauty in my house all fall long.

October 12

Cucamonga

Wilderness

We brought home

lots of bright

leaves. I found one

that is yellow, red,

and green!

WHAT YOU NEED:

bag or basket for leaf
    collecting
bleached beeswax or
    paraffin
double boiler (or a metal
    or glass bowl that
    stacks on top of a
    saucepan)
tweezers

WHAT TO DO:

1. Collect a variety of bright fall leaves. Choose different shapes, sizes, and colors.
2. With an adult's help, melt the wax slowly over a double boiler until fully melted.
3. Choose your first leaf and hold the stem with tweezers. Slowly dip the leaf into the wax, covering it completely.
4. Lift the leaf from the wax and gently shake off the extra.
5. To dry, lay the leaf on waxed paper. Or hang it on a string with a clothespin. Be sure to put something, like a paper towel or paper bag, underneath to catch the drips.
6. When your leaves have dried, decorate your house with fall's beauty. String the leaves into a garland, display them in a pretty bowl, or lay them out on a table. Now you have a beautiful keepsake of fall memories.

CLIMB TO NEW HEIGHTS

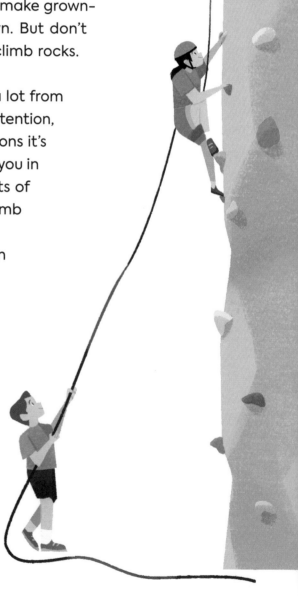

It's exciting to climb up a big rock. At each spot your fingers and toes find places to grip. Then, when you've made it to the top, you look down. You're so high up! Sometimes that can make grown-ups nervous. And they might ask you to get down. But don't worry! There are a lot of grown-ups who love to climb rocks. They can teach you how to climb safely.

Rock climbing is not an easy sport. It requires a lot from you. You need balance, endurance, calm nerves, attention, strength, and courage. But those are also the reasons it's so good to learn to rock climb. Those skills will help you in all parts of your life. Be sure to remind your parents of that when you tell them that you want to learn to climb big rocks!

With some planning and a lot of practice, you can become a rock-climbing expert.

WHAT TO DO:

Sign up for a rock-climbing class.

- Find a gym, outdoor store, or group near you that teaches rock climbing. There are different kinds of rock-climbing classes. There are indoor classes at a gym and outdoor classes on real rocks. There are also bouldering classes, rappelling classes, and safety-and-rescue classes.

- Choose a beginner class, even if you have gone rock climbing on your own.

- Make a plan to pay for the class. You might need to save up your own money, do extra chores, or ask for a class as a gift.

Attend the class.

- Learn how to safely wear and fasten the gear your instructor shows you. You'll learn how to tie a few kinds of knots. You'll need to know how to fasten your harness. And you'll find out how to move the rope to belay a climber. *Belay* means to stand on the ground and hold a climber's rope to keep them from falling.

- Watch your instructor demonstrate how to climb up and down.

- Ask questions! The instructor is there to guide you.

- When it's time to practice, do your best. Ask for help if you need it.

Practice.

- Practice tying the knots at home until you become an expert.

- Take another class. If you've only tried indoor climbing, take an outdoor class.

- Keep climbing!

TAKE A RIDE

Getting places in a different way can be a fun adventure. The first time I took my kids on a subway, they cheered when it went underground. They had never experienced anything like a subway because they'd only ridden in cars. It was exciting to read the maps at the underground stations. We figured out what train to take next and made sure we got on the right one. The kids loved the *whoosh* of cold air that came through the tunnel when the subway car arrived or left. It was thrilling to spend our day getting around *underneath* the city.

If you're used to riding public transportation, try something different. If you're used to the bus, take a train to a nearby city. If you're used to the subway, take a bus.

WHAT TO DO:

1. Ask an adult to help you find a bus stop or train or subway station near you. This will be much easier if you live in or near the city. If you live away from a city, you might have to drive a while to get to one of these stops. Your public transportation adventure will be a little longer!

2. Figure out where you'd like to go. You could plan to visit a city museum, park, or cultural area. Find out which route to take to get to your destination and what times the vehicles come and go.

3. On the day of your adventure, pack a backpack with a jacket, a water bottle, and some snacks. It's good to have these things while you are waiting for the bus or train. Walk or drive to the stop nearest you and wait for your ride to arrive.

4. Have fun experiencing the city in a new way.

5. Be sure to get back to the stop or station at the right time to catch your ride back home.

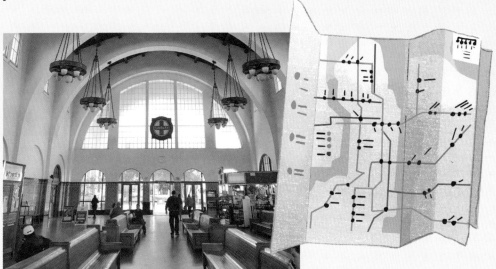

CONDUCT YOURSELF TO A SYMPHONY CONCERT

Do you know how many different musicians play together in one symphony orchestra? At least fifty musicians and as many as two hundred! The musicians play all kinds of different musical instruments, but together they play one beautiful piece of music.

BEFORE YOU GO:

- Find out if your town or a nearby city has its own symphony. If there isn't a professional orchestra where you live, look for a community symphony or high school or college symphony orchestra.

- Find the schedule for the orchestra on their website and plan which performance to attend. If you're seeing a professional orchestra, go to a morning or afternoon concert. Those tickets often cost less, and the concerts don't last as long.

- Learn about the instruments. Find out their names and sounds. A fun introduction to some of the symphony instruments is the story "Peter and the Wolf" by Sergei Prokofiev. You can listen to this musical fairy tale online!

- Listen to classical music. Try Ludwig van Beethoven, Claude Debussy, Aaron Copland, Camille Saint-Saëns, and John Williams.

- Find out what pieces the symphony will be performing. Listen to them ahead of time. You will enjoy the performance more if you are familiar with the music.

AT THE CONCERT:

- Arrive early so you can watch the orchestra warm up.

- Look for the instruments you know.

- Look for new instruments you don't recognize.

- Listen carefully and think about all the sounds. Do you notice any differences between hearing music live and hearing the recorded version at home? Which do you prefer?

KEEP LEARNING:

- Listen to more composers. Which ones are your favorites?

- Read books about the lives and works of those composers.

- Learn to play an instrument yourself!

GET FIRED UP

uilding a campfire is a great part of any outdoor adventure. Whether you are camping, backpacking, or just roasting s'mores in your backyard, having a good campfire adds excitement to your experience. Campfires provide heat, a way to cook food, light, and protection from wild animals.

SAFETY FIRST!

- Check fire regulations and make sure campfires are allowed where you are.

  - If there is a designated area to build a campfire, such as a metal grate or stone circle, use it.

    - If you have to make your own fire area, choose a dirt area away from all brush, trees, and other plants. Place rocks in a ring around your fire area.

      - Clear the fire area of dry grass, leaves, and sticks.

GATHER THE FUEL.

You need three kinds of material to fuel your fire:

1. **Tinder** is the stuff that starts the fire. It lights easily and burns fast. Use dry leaves, grass, bark, or pine needles for your tinder.
2. **Kindling** keeps your fire going before you put the big logs on. Use small, dry sticks or twigs for kindling. They should be about as big around as a pencil.
3. **Firewood** keeps your fire burning. Choose dry logs that are about as thick as your arm. Giant logs will smother your fire.

BUILD THE CAMPFIRE.

Building a fire that will quickly light and stay lit requires using a system. One of the easiest systems is called the "teepee."

1. In the center of your fire ring, make a small pile of tinder.
2. Over the tinder, lean the kindling against each other at the top to make a teepee shape.
3. With an adult's help, light the fire with a long-handled lighter or match.
4. Once the fire is burning strong, add the firewood a little at a time.

PUT THE FIRE OUT.

The best and safest way to put out a fire is to use water. Dirt or sand can keep the coals hot.

1. Let your fire burn down as much as possible.
2. Slowly pour water on the fire. Pour away from you so the steam doesn't burn you.
3. Stir the ashes with a long stick and keep pouring water until the fire is out.
4. Only leave your fire when you are certain the fire and embers are completely out. The ash should be cool to the touch.

PLAN A BOOK CLUB

A book club will take your book adventures to the next level. You can talk about books with your friends and even have book-themed parties.

WHAT TO DO:

1. **Pick a book.** Choose a book you've already read and loved or a new book. Just make sure it isn't too long or difficult to read, so that everyone in the club can enjoy it.

2. **Invite members.** Keep your group small if you are holding the club by yourself. If an adult wants to help, invite your friends and their siblings to make a bigger group.

   Send out an email invitation and let everyone know what book you'll be reading and when your first meeting and book celebration will be. Choose a date for the first celebration when everyone will have had time to read the book. Our book club reads four books a year, so we have a celebration meeting about every three months.

3. **Plan a book celebration.** A book celebration is an awesome kind of book club meeting! Each celebration will be different because each book is different.

CHOOSE THREE OR FOUR ACTIVITIES FOR EACH BOOK CELEBRATION:

Costumes—Dress up like characters from the book or from the time period of the setting.

Food—While reading the book, keep a list of the foods mentioned. Ask club members to sign up to bring a food from the list.

Discussion—Plan discussion questions ahead of time. Choose some easy questions and some more complicated questions.

Games, activities, or crafts—Some books include activities in the story. We've added things like leather working, a treasure hunt, a musical parade, new foods, and field games to our book celebrations.

Several weeks before the celebration, ask the members to help with food or activities. Email a sign-up sheet or ask certain people to do things you know they'll be good at.

When it's time to read the next book, let another member choose it and plan the celebration.

KNEAD TO BAKE BREAD

There are not many things I love more than the smell and taste of just-baked bread. It's hard to wait and let it cool before I cut it!

There are two kinds of bread: yeasted breads and quick breads. Yeasted breads use yeast to make the bread get fluffy, which is called *rising*. Quick breads use baking soda and baking powder to rise quickly.

If you've never made bread before, try a quick bread first. Pumpkin bread is a perfect choice for autumn. Next, try a yeast bread recipe.

RUSTIC YEAST BREAD

What you need:

3 ³/4 cups all-purpose flour

1 ¹/2 teaspoons kosher salt or fine sea salt

1 package quick-rise yeast

1 ¹/2 cups warm water

What to do:

1. Measure the flour, salt, and yeast into a large bowl. Mix well.
2. Add the warm water. Mix until all the ingredients come together in a thick, sticky dough with no dry flour left.
3. Cover the bowl with a kitchen towel. Set it in a warm place to rise for 30–45 minutes, until it is doubled in size.

4. Line a baking sheet with parchment paper. Dust your hands and the top of the loaf with flour. Gently pull the dough away from the sides of the bowl and into your hands. Shape the dough into a smooth ball.

5. Place the dough on the baking sheet. Cover with the towel. Let rise a second time until doubled in size—about 1 hour.

6. While the dough is rising, preheat your oven to 375 degrees.

7. Dust the top of the loaf with a little more flour. Bake for 45 minutes to 1 hour until the bread is golden brown.

8. Remove from the oven and place on a wire rack. Cool 1 hour before slicing.

ADAPTED FROM BAKERBETTIE.COM.

PUMPKIN BREAD

What you need:

1 15-ounce can of pumpkin puree
1/2 cup melted butter
3 large eggs
1 2/3 cups + 1 tablespoon sugar
1 1/2 teaspoons baking powder
3/4 teaspoon baking soda
3/4 teaspoon salt
3/4 teaspoon + 1 teaspoon ground cinnamon
1/4 teaspoon nutmeg
1/4 teaspoon ground ginger
1/4 teaspoon ground cloves
2 1/4 cups all-purpose flour

What to do:

1. Heat oven to 350 degrees.

2. Place the pumpkin puree, butter, eggs, and 1 2/3 cups sugar in a mixing bowl. Whisk until smooth.

3. Add baking powder, baking soda, salt, 3/4 teaspoon cinnamon, nutmeg, ginger, and cloves. Whisk until fully blended. Add the flour and stir with a spoon until fully mixed in.

4. Spray a 6-cup loaf pan with oil. Pour in the batter and smooth the top. Mix 1 tablespoon of sugar with 1 teaspoon of ground cinnamon. Sprinkle over the top of the bread.

5. Bake for 35 minutes. Turn the pan halfway around for even baking. Bake for another 30 to 40 minutes. When the loaf is done, a toothpick or knife inserted in the middle will come out clean. Let the bread cool completely in the pan. Then remove and slice.

ADAPTED FROM SMITTENKITCHEN.COM.

PICK AND DRY APPLES

Apple picking is a perfect fall adventure. At the orchard, we explore the trees that are bending under their load of bright, juicy apples. After we've filled our baskets, we make a jug of cold, refreshing cider on the apple press. When we get home, we make other treats with our apples: apple crisp, apple muffins, apple pie, caramel apples, and applesauce. There are so many yummy treats to make with apples.

Another treat we make is dried apples. In the days before refrigerators, apples were a perfect fruit because they stay fresh for a long time. People stored them in their cool, dark cellars. And even after the fruit started to get soft or go bad, the apples could be dried to last even longer. Plus, dried apples are sweet and delicious!

DRIED APPLES

What you need:

2 large fresh apples
4 cups water
1/2 cup lemon juice
cinnamon (optional)

What to do:

1. Turn on the oven to 200 degrees. (Ask an adult for help with the oven.)
2. Wash the apples.
3. Slice off the tops and bottoms of the apples. Then cut them into thin, round slices.
4. Combine the water and lemon juice in a large bowl. Dip the apple slices in the lemon water. Be sure to cover them completely.
5. Lay the slices on a clean kitchen towel and pat them dry.
6. Cover a cookie sheet in parchment paper. Lay the apples on the sheet in one layer.
7. Sprinkle with cinnamon if you want cinnamon apples.
8. Bake for 1 hour.
9. Turn each apple slice over. Bake for 1 more hour for soft, chewy apples. Bake 2 more hours if you'd like crispy apple slices.
10. Turn off the oven and prop the oven door open. Let the apples cool 1 1/2 to 2 hours.
11. Enjoy your old-fashioned treat!

DARE TO TRY

We all have things we'd like to learn to do but are a little scared to try. It might be singing in front of a group of people, riding a unicycle, or sewing. It can be hard or frustrating to learn a new skill, even if you are really serious about it. You might even think to yourself, *What if I can't do it?* But be brave. And persistent. You can learn new things!

Mark the activities you'd like to try. Then add some of your own ideas.

THINGS I WANT TO TRY

☐ MAKE BALLOON ANIMALS.
☐ RIDE A HORSE.
☐ HIT A BASEBALL.
☐ MAKE SUSHI.
☐ JUGGLE.
☐ READ A MAP.
☐ DO A HANDSTAND.
☐ MAKE POTTERY.

☐ MAKE A MEAL BY MYSELF.
☐ FIX A FLAT TIRE ON MY BIKE.
☐ WRITE CALLIGRAPHY.
☐ PITCH A TENT.
☐ DRAW PORTRAITS.
☐ USE A SEWING MACHINE.
☐ RIDE A BIKE.

Now look at the things you chose. Which one seems easiest? Try it now! As your confidence and courage grow, try the other things on your list.

ROCKS, GEMS, AND MINERALS, OH MY!

When I was growing up, we had a big hill behind our house that was pretty much made of rocks. I loved to take a bag, a small hammer, and a shovel and spend hours on that hill digging up rocks. I pretended I was a miner as I filled my bag with dusty pieces of quartz. I planned to polish up my rocks and sell them to world-class museums and rock stores for gazillions of dollars.

Guess what? I still love collecting rocks. My pockets and backpack often have rocks in them from my latest hike. My family's washing machine and dryer often have rocks tumbling around in them because someone forgot to empty their pockets. And we have jars full of special, interesting, and beautiful rocks around the house because they just make us happy.

To discover more of these amazing underground things, go rock hunting.

- Look for a museum in your area with a rock collection. Sometimes these are small museums. Or a natural history museum might have a special rock section. If you can't find a museum, look for shops or shows that specialize in rocks, gems, and minerals. Museum, shop, and show exhibits will have the most incredible and hard-to-find pieces.

- Learn the name of your state's rock and where it can be found. Plan an outing to see formations of the state rock.

- Research the other types of rocks where you live. Make yourself a local guidebook to the rocks, gems, and minerals in your area with pictures, names, and facts.

- Find a site where your local rocks might be found and go for a dig!

DEEP SEA SIGHTSEEING

Scientists know of about thirty-four thousand types of fish in the world. But they also believe there are many fish that haven't even been discovered yet. And that's just the fish! There are many other creatures that live in the ocean, from the tiniest plankton to the giant squid. And there are sea otters, walruses, and lobsters in between.

Unfortunately, most ocean animals live deep under water, so we don't get to see them. Unless we visit an aquarium! At an aquarium, you can get up close with fish and other sea creatures that you might not ever get to see otherwise.

Aquariums are all over the country. Many big cities have large aquariums that take a whole day to visit. Smaller towns sometimes have aquariums too, especially if they're close to the ocean. Zoos often have aquatic areas where you can see ocean animals. You can also visit the fish section at a pet store or find an outdoor recreation store that has an aquarium display.

BEFORE YOU GO:

- Think of your favorite fish and sea animals. Research whether they live at the aquarium you are visiting.

- Pack your nature journal and art supplies so you can do some drawings while you are there.

WHAT TO DO AT THE AQUARIUM:

1. Get a map and locate your favorite animals. Sit in those exhibits and take your time watching. Many sea creatures spend most of their life hiding, so be patient and look carefully.
2. When you find the animals, study what they look like and how they move. Then draw them.
3. Read signs to learn fun facts about the animals. Jot down the things you want to remember next to your drawings.
4. Explore the rest of the aquarium. Are there animals you didn't know about? Pick one and make a page in your journal about it.

DISCOVER NATIONAL TREASURES

Most of us have heard of national parks and maybe even visited one. But there are many kinds of places that the government protects because they are important to our nation.

National sites can be natural places like rock formations, volcanoes, forests, bodies of water, and wildlife reserves. They can also be places where history happened, like statues, battlefields and battleships, art pieces, historic buildings, and lighthouses.

September 5

Devil's Tower National Monument, Wyoming

Devil's Tower looks so weird! It shoots straight out of the flat ground. I like the legend that it was made by a giant bear's claws. The bear's claws would have to be huge to form those ridges!

BEFORE YOU GO:

1. Do an online search for "national protected site near me." There are sites in every state.
2. Look for places that are natural and places that are historical. Plan to visit one of each kind.
3. Learn about each site. Visit its website or borrow a book about it from the library. Find out the site's history and what makes it special.

AT THE SITE:

1. Start at the visitor's center, ranger station, or entry sign. Get a map or brochure to learn everything you can see on your visit. If there is an exhibit or film, be sure to view it.
2. Take your time touring the site.
3. Sketch your favorite parts in your journal. You can also bring home a map or brochure and cut and paste pictures into your journal.

MAKE A FALL NATURE COLLECTION

When the seasons change, it's time to put away your summer items and begin to fill your nature collection with beautiful fall treasures. Brightly colored fall leaves are probably the most perfect addition to a nature collection. I like to press them flat between the pages of a book or dip them in wax to preserve them.

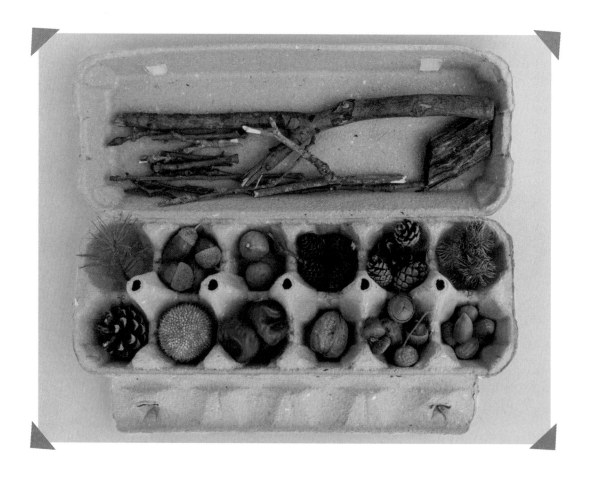

LOOK FOR THESE OTHER FALL ITEMS TO ADD TO YOUR COLLECTION:

acorns and other nuts
seed pods
flowers that have dried on their stalks
pine cones
gourds
shed skins of lizards and snakes
molted exoskeletons of bugs

WHAT TO DO:

1. Decide on a place to keep your nature finds. You might use a shelf in your room or in the living room if your parents say it's okay. You could also use a shoe box or a drawer in your dresser. You'll also need a small notebook to keep with your collection to record your finds.
2. Look for special nature items every time you go outside. Make sure it's okay to take the item home.
3. In your notebook, identify what the item is, the date you found it, and where you found it. If you don't know what it is, do research to identify it. If your items are displayed on a shelf, you can make labels for each item with the same information.
4. If you go on a fall trip, bring your notebook and a sturdy container to keep your items safe while you are traveling.

To mix up your collection each season, think of new ways to display your items. A waxed leaf garland or a dried flower bouquet are great ways to display fall items.

POET PRACTICE: FALL

There are so many fun and beautiful poems about fall! One of my favorites is "September" by Helen Hunt Jackson. You can memorize this nature poem and make an art project with it.

WHAT TO DO:

1. This poem describes many autumn plants and flowers. Are there any you recognize? Which ones are new to you? Find them online or in books to see what they look like.
2. Read the poem again and picture each plant.
3. Print or write a copy of the poem. Add drawings of all the flowers and plants as a border around the poem.
4. Read the poem every day until you have it memorized.

September

The goldenrod is yellow;
The corn is turning brown;
The trees in apple orchards
With fruit are bending down.

The gentian's* bluest fringes
Are curling in the sun;
In dusky pods the milkweed
Its hidden silk has spun.

The sedges flaunt their harvest
In every meadow-nook;
And asters by the brookside
Make asters in the brook.

From dewy lanes at morning
The grapes' sweet odors rise;
At noon the roads all flutter
With yellow butterflies.

By all these lovely tokens
September days are here,
With summer's best of weather,
And autumn's best of cheer.

But none of all this beauty
Which floods the earth and air
Is unto me the secret
Which makes September fair.

'Tis a thing which I remember;
To name it thrills me yet:
One day of one September
I never can forget.

—Helen Hunt Jackson
from *Poems*, 1893

*gentian: say *jen-shun*

RAINY-DAY RAMBLE

Hiking in the rain may sound strange, but it can be a great way to explore the outdoors. Nature looks, smells, sounds, and feels different when it is raining. All you need is the right gear and an adventurous spirit.

WHAT YOU NEED:

- rain jacket or poncho
- waterproof or breathable, quick-drying shoes with good grip on the soles
- extra pair of dry socks
- water
- thermos of a warm drink
- snacks that are easy to eat, such as granola bars, nuts, fruit leather, jerky, and even a chocolate bar or cookie for a treat
- waterproof cover for your pack or one made from a trash bag
- waterproof pants (optional)
- big trash bags for your wet gear when you return to your car
- old towels to sit on for the drive home

WHAT TO DO:

1. Find a trail that will make a good rainy-day hike. Some trails close when it rains because of the danger of wet conditions or because people walking on the wet trail can cause damage. Look for a trail without a lot of hills that will be slippery. Plan to hike in the woods. The trees will provide protection from the rain as you hike. Also, find a trail without stream crossings. Streams can get swollen with rain and make them difficult or even dangerous to cross.

2. As you hike, take your time. Rainy-day hikes aren't meant to be hiked fast.

3. Stop and listen to the sounds of the rain falling. The drops will sound different falling on the trees, on a pond or stream, or on an open trail. Which one is your favorite?

4. Look for animals, birds, or insects that come out in the rain.

5. Observe the way the plants respond to the rain. Are they limp and soggy? Or do they hold their leaves open wide to accept the drink from the sky?

6. When you return to your car, put all your wet gear in the trash bags to keep the car clean and dry.

7. Give your adult an extra thank-you for taking you on this rainy-day adventure.

HAWK-EYED HOBBY

One of my favorite books when I was growing up was *My Side of the Mountain.* It's about a boy named Sam who has a pet peregrine falcon named Frightful. Sam captured his falcon in the wild when she was just a baby, then trained her to be his pet. Sam taught Frightful to ride on his shoulder and to hunt for him. Training a bird of prey like this is called *falconry*. I loved reading about Sam and Frightful's adventures together.

But you don't have to be a falconer to see falcons, hawks, and eagles soaring and diving. Grab a pair of binoculars and head outside to spot some birds of prey performing air acrobatics. Whether you live in the city, country, or somewhere in between, birds of prey are not far away.

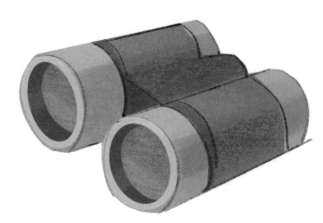

WHAT TO DO:

1. Research which birds of prey are most common in your area. Print pictures of them or get a bird field guide.
2. Find out where these birds live in your area. Birds of prey can be found around water, around forests, in open spaces like grassland and deserts, in neighborhoods, in parks, and even around tall city buildings.
3. Bring binoculars and your nature journal and go to the site.
4. Sit still and wait for the birds to make their appearance.
5. When you see one, try to identify it with your pictures or guide.
6. Take a picture if you can get one.
7. Write down the name of the bird and draw a picture in your nature journal.

Continue going to different places where birds of prey might live near your home. How many kinds of birds can you find?

FIELD GUIDE TO BIRDS

THE TASTE OF FALL

One autumn day in the grocery store, my kids and I counted sixty-four pumpkin spice–flavored items. There were cookies, drinks, chips, candy, soup, and so many other things. We thought it was a little crazy. But people really love pumpkin-flavored foods in the fall.

I like to cook or bake something with a real pumpkin at least once every autumn. I don't like cleaning the seeds out of a pumpkin, but I do love to roast them. Freshly roasted pumpkin seeds are nutty and salty and delicious! And it's fun to cook a pumpkin until it's nice and soft and then make our own bright orange pumpkin puree instead of spooning it out of a can. Because it's so fresh, you'll find it has a richer, more pumpkiny taste. A taste of fall!

ROASTED PUMPKIN

What you need:

sugar pumpkin (also
   called a pie pumpkin)
large metal spoon
large bowl of water
large cookie sheet
parchment paper
blender or food
   processor

What to do:

1. Wash the pumpkin and cut it in half from top to bottom through the stem.
2. With a large metal spoon, scoop out the seeds and long stringy pieces of pith. Set the seeds aside in a bowl of water to clean and roast later.
3. Line a cookie sheet with parchment paper. Lay the pumpkin halves cut side down.
4. Roast at 375 degrees for an hour or until the halves pierce easily with a knife.
5. Remove the pumpkin from the oven. Let it cool until you can handle it comfortably.
6. With the spoon, scrape the cooked pumpkin from the skin into a food processor or blender.
7. Blend the cooked pumpkin until smooth.

PUMPKIN TREATS

Now you can use your pumpkin puree for all kinds of yummy treats! Which one will you choose?

pumpkin pie
pumpkin scones
pumpkin pasta
pumpkin cheesecake
pumpkin butter
pumpkin soup
pumpkin donuts

pumpkin oatmeal
pumpkin smoothies
pumpkin pancakes
pumpkin spice cake
pumpkin pizza
pumpkin mousse
pumpkin ice cream

pumpkin bread
See a recipe for pumpkin bread in Activity 33.

A FAIRLY CRAFTY AFFAIR

Making crafts is a lot of fun. Sharing your crafts is even better. A great way to do that is by hosting a craft fair. You and your friends can display your crafts and buy and sell them or trade them with one another. You can even invite family, neighbors, and other friends to come shop. You might like hosting the craft fair so much that you make it an annual event.

Tip: Consider having the fair about a month before Christmas so people can buy crafted holiday gifts and decor.

CRAFT IDEAS

- sewn or knitted items
- baked goods
- soap
- candles
- jams and jellies
- balloon art
- jewelry
- art
- fresh-picked fruits or vegetables
- wooden cars, swords, or other handmade toys
- face painting
- flower arrangements

WHAT TO DO:

Plan

1. Pick a day for your craft fair that is about three months in the future. That gives everyone plenty of time to make their crafts.
2. Choose a location for the fair, such as a park or church gym. Be sure to check with the organization in charge of the space, such as your city's parks department, to find out whether you need to make a reservation.
3. Decide whether crafts will be for sale, for trading, or both.
4. Send out an email sign-up sheet for crafters. Include the date, start and end times, location, and due date for signing up. Let people know if they can sell their crafts, trade them, or both. Also tell them to bring a table or blanket to display their crafts. Lastly, give them some ideas for crafts they can bring to the craft fair.
5. Make invitations for fair visitors. You can send an email to your church, school group, friends, and family. Send out the invitations about a month before the event, with a reminder the week before. You can also print flyers to hand out.
6. Make a sign to tell people passing by about the awesome craft fair going on—you might just get more visitors!

On Fair Day

1. Arrive early. Put out your sign.
2. Set up your crafts.
3. Walk around and look at the crafts your friends have made.
4. Buy, sell, and trade crafts.
5. When it is time to go home, clean up the fair site. Leave it better than you found it.

BUILD AN OUTDOOR FORT

My favorite places when I was a kid were my tree forts. I had a few different forts that my dad built for me, and I loved them all. I kept them clean, sweeping every day. I brought in old blankets and pillows to make the floors comfy for sitting. In one of them, I even had a beanbag chair. I loved to bring a snack up to the tree fort and spend the afternoon in my beanbag with a book.

I liked to make other forts too: in the tall grass of the empty field across the street, in a bare spot between the bushes next to the neighbor's house, and down by the fruit trees where I could eat ripe fruit whenever I got hungry. Those forts weren't permanent, and they weren't fancy. But I loved creating a place of my own in the outdoors. A place where I could read and draw and pretend and just be.

You can build an outdoor fort to create your own special space.

WHAT YOU NEED:

old blankets or sheets
rope or twine
clothespins or big binder
**   clips**
old tree branches (optional;
**   they help shape the fort)**
large rocks or bricks

WHAT TO DO:

1. Find a good place for your fort. You can build your fort anywhere outside like in a tree, under a bush, next to a fence or rock wall, or in grass.

2. Lay a sheet or blanket on the ground. Place rocks or bricks at the corners if it's windy.

3. Make a roof. Tie the rope between trees or lean logs against each other and lay a blanket across the top. Or try clipping the blanket to a tree, bush, or fence. Secure the blanket to the ground with rocks. You can also have a fort with no roof except the sky.

ENJOY THE FORT

- DRAW, PAINT, OR WRITE IN YOUR NATURE JOURNAL.
- READ A BOOK.
- TAKE A NAP.
- INVITE YOUR BROTHER OR SISTER IN TO PLAY CARDS WITH YOU.
- BIRD-WATCH WITH BINOCULARS.
- SNUGGLE WITH YOUR DOG OR CAT OR STUFFED ANIMAL.

Activity 46

GARDEN IN A JAR

A terrarium is a mini garden you can keep in your house. It's a closed glass container with plants inside. But the cool thing about a terrarium is that it waters the plants itself. Water evaporates from the plants, and droplets build up on the walls of the container. Then the droplets run back down the walls, watering the plants inside. A terrarium creates its own miniature rain cycle!

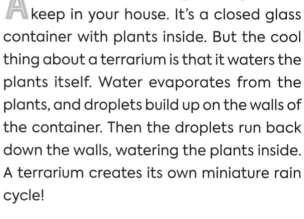

WHAT YOU NEED:

large, clear-glass container with a lid
small stones or pebbles
activated charcoal
potting soil
small plants that like humidity
spray bottle

WHAT TO DO:

1. Cover the bottom of the terrarium with a layer of pebbles about 1 ½ inches thick.
2. Add a ½-inch layer of activated charcoal.
3. Add a 2-inch layer of potting soil.
4. Arrange the plants one at a time, nestling them gently into the potting soil.
5. Gently mist the soil and plants.
6. Cover the soil with moss or pebbles.
7. Close the terrarium. Place it in indirect sunlight, such as in a window that faces east or north.
8. Check on your terrarium every couple of days. The sides and top should get misty under bright light. If no moisture collects, spray the plants and soil. If the glass becomes cloudy, open the lid for a few hours. The extra moisture will evaporate. Once you get the right balance of moisture, your terrarium will mostly take care of itself.

CHALK UP A SMILE

Have you ever gotten a surprise that made you smile? Maybe it was a present left at your door or finding that one of your chores was already done. Maybe you didn't even know who gave you the surprise!

You can create your own sneaky surprise of kindness by leaving an encouraging chalk message on your sidewalk or driveway. When people pass by, they will bump into a surprise smile!

WHAT YOU NEED:

- encouraging quote or Bible verse
- a section of concrete you're allowed to draw on
- sidewalk chalk

WHAT TO DO:

1. Choose a quote. Print it or write it down.
2. In giant letters, copy the encouraging words onto the concrete.
3. Add colorful designs around the words.
4. Go inside and watch for people's smiles when they see your message.

EXAMPLE QUOTES

Hold fast to hope.
Leave a sparkle wherever you go.
Be awesome today!
Never lose your sense of wonder.

Be kind to one another.
You are an adventure story.
You are wonderful!
You brighten the day.
You are courageous!
You are loved.

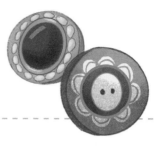

CREATE A COLLECTION

When I was in fourth grade, I started a stamp collection. I soon had stamps from far-off countries, and I pasted them in an album. I went to stamp-collecting shows and met people who had been collecting stamps much longer than I had. They shared stamps with me and told me stories about where they found them. I still have some of my stamp albums, and I love looking at them even now.

Collecting things can be its own kind of adventure. You get to become an expert at something. And it introduces you to new people and places.

WHAT TO DO:

1. Read the collection idea list below and check off the things you are interested in collecting.
2. See if you already have some of the items. If you do, that's the start of your collection!
3. Learn about the item you are collecting. Where does it come from? What is it made of? What is its purpose?
4. Be on the lookout for new items for your collection. Ask friends and relatives to help you gather items.
5. Visit shows, fairs, or stores and see other people's collections.
6. Share your collection with others.

TYPES OF COLLECTIONS

buttons

pencils

magnets

sports cards

patches

foreign coins

snow globes

Lego mini figures

salt and pepper
    shakers

Christmas tree
    ornaments

mini erasers

smashed pennies

Pez dispensers

Matchbox cars

rocks and shells

bird nests

dried flowers and
    leaves

LEARN TO HAND STITCH

Knowing how to sew by hand is a fun and helpful skill to have. You can sew on a button that comes off your coat. You can put a patch on your backpack or stitch a gift for a friend. You can also learn to make cross-stitch pictures, embroider your name on a shirt, or make a quilt.

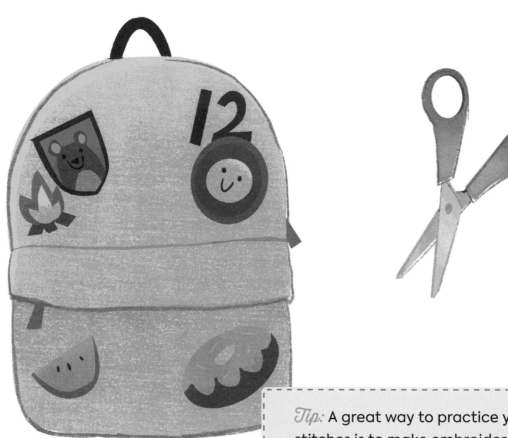

Tip: A great way to practice your stitches is to make embroidered pictures. Do an online search for "easy embroidery pattern for kids" to find fun pictures you can sew!

WHAT YOU NEED:

needle with a large eye
embroidery thread
scissors
pieces of thick fabric,
    such as felt

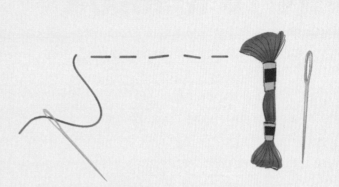

Learn your first stitch.

The most basic stitch is the straight stitch, also called the running stitch.

1. Thread your needle and knot one end of the thread.
2. Poke the needle through the fabric, from bottom to top. Pull the thread through until the knot catches.
3. Poke the needle back through the fabric, from top to bottom. Pull the needle and thread through.
4. Repeat steps 2 and 3 to form a line of stitches.
5. Tie off by making a double knot on the underside of the fabric.

Learn other stitches.

Once you feel comfortable with a straight stitch, learn some others by watching online videos.

☐ BLANKET STITCH   ☐ OVERSTITCH   ☐ CHAIN STITCH
☐ FRENCH KNOT   ☐ BACKSTITCH   ☐ SATIN STITCH

WRITE TO A SOLDIER

When my dad was nineteen years old, he joined the army. While he was in training, he injured his knee and had to have surgery. It was Christmas, and he lay alone in a hospital bed far away from his family and friends. It was a tough time for him, but there was one bright spot in his days. He received letters from children he didn't even know. "Dear soldier, my name is . . ." they all began. My dad is sixty-eight years old now, and he still has those letters. They are very special to him.

Veterans Day is a perfect time to send letters to soldiers. The holiday is on November 11, and it's all about thanking veterans for their service to our country. Invite your family to join you and send letters to soldiers who need some cheer.

WHAT TO DO:

- If you know someone serving in the military, ask his or her family for their address.

- If you don't know a serviceperson, find an organization that sends mail to these soldiers, such as Operation Gratitude, Soldiers' Angels, and Forgotten Soldiers Outreach.

- To begin your letter, introduce yourself with your name, where you live, and your family members.

- Describe what you like to do for fun.

- Ask the soldier questions about themselves in case they want to write back.

- Include a photo of yourself or your family.

- Draw a picture to brighten the walls of their locker or barracks.

- Most of all, be sure to thank them for their service to our country and to you and your family.

Writing a letter is an easy thing to do, but it will surely brighten a soldier's day!

WALK IN A WINTER WONDERLAND

ANIMAL DIORAMA DRAMA

TASTE TEST

SNOW-WHITE CANVAS

SEE *THE NUTCRACKER* BALLET

BAKE AND TAKE

BOOK NOOK

START SEEDS

CELEBRATE THE SOLSTICE

OUTER SPACE ON THE CEILING

WINTER ADVENTURES

FEED THE BIRDS

WINTER SCAVENGING

DEAR PEN PAL

GINGERBREAD CONSTRUCTION

POET PRACTICE: WINTER

CREATE YOUR STATE

SNOWY NIGHT

ART ALIVE

LOOK FOR LICHEN

MAKE A STICK MOBILE

MAKE STAMPED VALENTINES

START AN ADVENTURE JOURNAL

SNOW CASTLE

DESIGN A HABITAT DIORAMA

PARTY AROUND THE WORLD

WALK IN A WINTER WONDERLAND

The glitter of everything covered with snow. Hot cocoa in a thermos. The perfectly stamped shapes of animal footprints. Snowball fights. Hiking in the snow can feel like an adventure in a magical world.

Hiking in the cold and snow requires some extra preparation. But with a little planning, you'll have a special time walking in a winter wonderland!

Tip: If it's really cold, put your water bottle in a wool sock to keep it from freezing.

BE SAFE:

- Check the weather before you go. If it is snowing heavily, extremely cold, or hard to see, reschedule for another day.

- Never hike alone. It's especially important to hike with others in extreme weather.

WHERE TO HIKE:

- Find a trail that stays open in the winter and snow.

- Pick a trail that isn't too long or too icy.

- Avoid trails with water crossings, steep slopes that can avalanche, and steep drop-offs where you could slip over the edge.

- Hike when the sun and temperature are highest. Plan to finish your hike at least a couple of hours before sunset.

WHAT TO WEAR:

Dress in layers. You may not need everything at the start of the hike, or you may have to take some layers off as you warm up. But bring them in case the weather changes.

- **Base layer:** a thin, warm layer next to your skin
- **Mid-layer:** a fleece jacket or thin, insulated jacket and some pants that are extra thick or lined
- **Outer layer:** warm, waterproof pants and coat
- **Accessories:** warm hat, scarf, insulated gloves, and wool socks
- **Footwear:** warm, waterproof boots with good traction, snowshoes if there will be deep snow, or crampons or microspikes for ice

WHAT TO BRING:

- Backpack to carry your gear
- Water, plus an extra water bottle because it's easy to get dehydrated in cold temperatures
- Thermos with a warm drink like cocoa, tea, or broth
- Food you can eat while you walk, like energy bars, trail mix, chocolate, or jerky
- First aid kit
- Sunscreen to protect any exposed skin from the extra-strong sun bouncing off the snow
- Headlamp or flashlight (If you take longer than planned, a light will help you make it back safely in the dark.)

GINGERBREAD CONSTRUCTION

My family loves decorating gingerbread houses. But you know what? We cheat a little. We use graham crackers and hot glue instead of gingerbread and frosting! They hold together so much better. And they are much easier to decorate.

You can go two ways with gingerbread houses. You can create something you can eat later, which tends to be messier. Or you can make something sturdy that looks better. It's up to you!

> *Tip:* Let the houses dry completely after putting them together. If you're decorating with guests, either build all the houses ahead of time or plan an activity to do while you wait. You could watch a Christmas movie, play tag outside, or go for a nature walk.

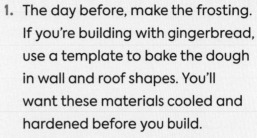

WHAT YOU NEED:

gingerbread, graham crackers, or cardboard for the house walls and roof

hot glue or thick frosting

clean cardboard pieces for the house bases

old sheet or tablecloth to work on

frosting and butter knives for decorating

icing bags and tips (optional)

candy and other treats for decorating

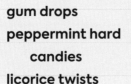

WHAT TO DO:

1. The day before, make the frosting. If you're building with gingerbread, use a template to bake the dough in wall and roof shapes. You'll want these materials cooled and hardened before you build.

2. Cover the table with a sheet or tablecloth.

3. For graham cracker or cardboard houses, make the wall and roof pieces. To cut the peaked walls from graham crackers, ask an adult to help you gently saw the angles with a sharp knife.

4. Use the hot glue or frosting to build a house on the cardboard base. Let dry.

5. Put out the bowls of candy and treats, frosting and butter knives, and filled icing bags and decorating tips.

6. Decorate!

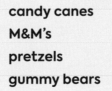

DECORATIONS

gum drops	candy canes	marshmallows
peppermint hard candies	M&M's	vanilla wafer cookies
licorice twists	pretzels	sprinkles
	gummy bears	Red Hots

SEE *THE NUTCRACKER* BALLET

One of the most famous ballets is a narrative ballet called *The Nutcracker*. Narrative ballets tell a story. But these ballets don't use words. Instead, the music and dancing show what happens to the characters. *The Nutcracker* is especially great if you aren't used to going to the ballet. It is beautiful, fun, and exciting. There's even an evil rat king and sword fighting!

BEFORE YOU GO:

- Learn the story of *The Nutcracker* by reading picture books.

- Listen to the music of *The Nutcracker* by the composer Tchaikovsky (say *Chai-koff-skee*).

- Learn what to expect at the ballet. Find out how long the performance will be. Learn where you'll sit and what kind of voice to use during the ballet.

- Pack a small snack and water bottle.

AT THE THEATER:

1. Visit the bathroom. Explore the lobby to get out some energy before the ballet begins.
2. Find your seats and watch the orchestra warm up.
3. When the show begins, listen for the music you know.
4. Watch and see how the story is told differently than in the books. What did the books leave out? What did they add?
5. During the intermission, get out of your seat. Get a drink of water, use the bathroom, and eat your snack. Don't forget to get all your wiggles out before the second half of the ballet!

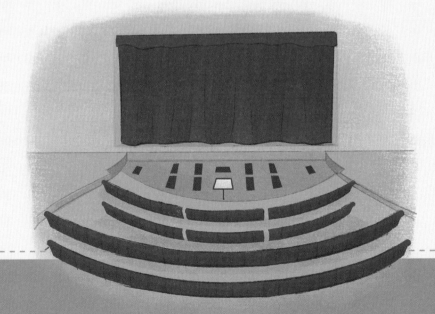

MAKE A STICK MOBILE

Sometimes there are more gray days in wintertime than sunshiney ones. But you can add brightness and cheer to your bedroom or home by creating a colorful stick mobile.

WHAT YOU NEED:

5 to 10 sticks of different sizes (Just make sure they will fit in your house!)

old tablecloth, sheet, or newspapers

washable paint and paintbrush

various colors of yarn or embroidery thread

WHAT TO DO:

1. Brush any dirt off your sticks. If they are wet, let them sit out to dry.
2. Cover your work area with something you can paint on. An old tablecloth, sheet, or newspapers are good choices.
3. Decide how you will decorate your sticks. You can paint each stick a single color. You can paint just the ends or the middle. You can paint designs like stripes and polka dots. Or paint anything you dream up. You can also wrap yarn around parts of a stick or a whole stick. Have fun and be creative!
4. Once you have a plan, paint the sticks.
5. After the paint is dry, add the yarn.
6. Figure out the arrangement of your mobile. Choose the largest stick for your top piece, medium sticks for the middle, and the smallest sticks for the bottom.
7. Tie a medium stick to the largest stick with yarn.
8. Add the other medium sticks. As you work, check your mobile's balance after every couple of sticks. You'll need to position the sticks so the large stick continues to hang straight. Take your time and get help if you need it.
9. Add the small sticks. Remember to check the balance and adjust after every couple of sticks.
10. Hang up your mobile. Enjoy the bright spot of color on gray winter days.

START AN ADVENTURE JOURNAL

Lots of people make resolutions for the New Year. Others make something called a bucket list or life list of all the things they want to do. Maybe they plan to volunteer or learn a new skill or travel to a new place. I like to dream of all the adventures I'll have that year.

Recently our family went on a great big adventure, and we each kept a journal of the trip. I enjoyed my journal so much that I started an adventure journal for the New Year. I started my journal with a list of ideas for adventures I wanted to take. Then each time my family went on an adventure, I made an entry—no matter how small the adventure was—even if it wasn't on my original list. I'll enjoy looking back at all of them when the year is done.

January 5

I want to ride a roller coaster this year. Maybe one that goes upside down!

PREPARE YOUR JOURNAL:

- Find a journal you like. I like spiral-bound notebooks because they lay flat, but you can use any kind of blank book.

- If the cover is blank, decorate it with stickers or art. If you have a designed cover, decorate the first page.

- Write your name on the journal.

- Write your hopes and dreams for adventures in the coming year. Do you hope to visit a waterfall, see a shooting star, or ride a roller coaster? Put those things in your journal.

- Return to the list throughout the year as you make adventure plans.

RECORD YOUR ADVENTURES:

- Include the date and place.

- Name who was there with you.

- Include some highlights of what you saw, ate, and did. Add any funny or exciting stories.

- Tape in stickers, postcards, nature finds, or pictures.

At the end of the year, go back to your hopes list. Which adventure dreams came true? Write the ones you didn't get to in a new section or new journal for the next year!

ANIMAL DIORAMA DRAMA

When the weather is yucky, we explore nature from inside the Natural History Museum in Los Angeles. We always head to the mammal halls first. In big rooms, floor-to-ceiling exhibits display various kinds of animals. The exhibits are called *dioramas*. Each diorama is a life-size scene of animals surrounded by their natural environment.

One diorama is home to a great, big grizzly bear, standing on his hind legs. He's so tall! You can see the size and sharpness of his claws and the black of his snout. Around him are the kind of trees, rocks, and water you'd find in Alaska where lots of grizzly bears live. And there is some food grizzly bears like too—berries, grubs, and fish. Each diorama gives you a glimpse into the world of that animal.

BEFORE YOU GO:

1. Find a natural history museum near you. If you can visit a large museum in a big city, you should! These museums have so many different animals on display. But you can also visit a smaller local museum or even a nature center near you. These places have wonderful animal exhibits on display too.
2. Plan a time to visit the museum.
3. Pack a small backpack. Bring a water bottle and snacks or a lunch. Pack your nature journal and your favorite pens or colored pencils.

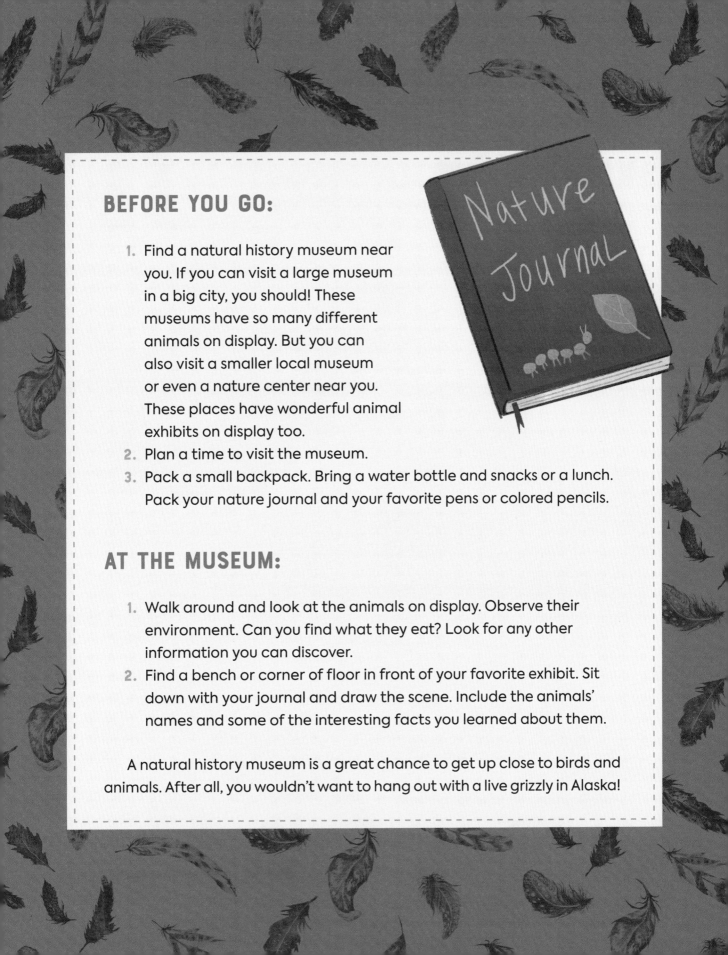

AT THE MUSEUM:

1. Walk around and look at the animals on display. Observe their environment. Can you find what they eat? Look for any other information you can discover.
2. Find a bench or corner of floor in front of your favorite exhibit. Sit down with your journal and draw the scene. Include the animals' names and some of the interesting facts you learned about them.

A natural history museum is a great chance to get up close to birds and animals. After all, you wouldn't want to hang out with a live grizzly in Alaska!

SNOWY NIGHT

I have always wanted to try snow camping. Even though it sounds really cold! But waking up to a snowy landscape outside my tent would be beautiful.
So I'd try snow camping. Would you?

WHAT YOU NEED:

four-season tent
sleeping bag for below-freezing
    temperatures
inflatable and insulated sleeping mat
snow shovel
camp stove and fuel
food and water
warm clothing:
    base layer, mid-layer, and outer layer
    warm, waterproof boots
    warm hat, scarf, and insulated gloves
    extra clothes and socks
waterproof bag
headlamp or flashlight and extra
    batteries
warmer packs for your feet, hands, or
    body (optional)
book, cards, or a game

CHOOSE A CAMPSITE:

Pick a campsite where you can pitch your tent next to your car and get water from a spigot or stream. It's also nice to have a camp store for firewood and hot cocoa. It's okay if you're not out in the wilderness. This is a great start to snow camping.

AT THE CAMPSITE:

- Find a level place to pitch your tent. Pack down the snow with your shovel. Make the area as large and flat as possible. Let the snow get hard before you put the tent on it.

- Cook your food on a camp stove. You might need to warm up the fuel canisters in your jacket or sleeping bag before using.

- For cooking water or hot drinks, melt snow over the fire. This will save stove fuel.

- At night, keep your boots in a waterproof bag at the bottom of your sleeping bag. If you don't, they'll be freezing in the morning! Also keep these other things in your sleeping bag overnight to keep them warm: gloves, hat, scarf, jacket, and water bottle.

- After dark, climb into your warm sleeping bag. Read a book or play a game.

- Keep a different bottle in your tent to use if you must go to the bathroom at night. Going outside or even to the campground bathroom can be very, very cold. Make sure the bathroom bottle is well marked. Research special tools to make it easy for a girl or boy camper to use.

BE SAFE!

- Always check the weather and road conditions before you leave. If the weather is going to be extremely cold or stormy, reschedule your trip.

- Don't let yourself get too cold. Go for a walk, do jumping jacks, or do sit-ups in your tent. Moving your body helps you warm up. You can also use warmer packs. These handy pads become hot when opened. They are great to put in your boots, gloves, or an inside pocket.

Activity 58

TASTE TEST

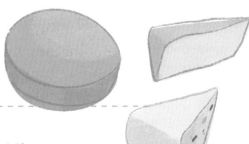

What's your favorite food? Do you remember the first time you tasted it? Trying new food is an easy way to have an adventure.

A wonderful place to go on this food adventure is a food hall. A food hall is a place where there are a bunch of small restaurants and shops that sell fresh produce, spices, cheese, and meat. They're all gathered in one place, so it's easy to do all your shopping or try several restaurants.

Some famous food halls you might have been to or heard of are Pike's Place in Seattle, the Original Farmers Market in Los Angeles, Chelsea Market in New York City, and Quincy Market in Boston. There are lots of smaller food halls too. Can you find one near you?

WHAT TO DO:

1. Find a food hall nearby. If you live in a small town, the farmers market is the next best thing.
2. Look up the restaurants or booths ahead of time to learn what kind of food they serve. Choose one new food to try on your visit. Encourage everyone who is going along to pick out a new food too.
3. When you get to the food hall, have everyone order their food and then meet at a table. Share all the food to have an even bigger food adventure.
4. Talk about the foods you liked and didn't like.

What will you order on your next food adventure?

BOOK NOOK

One of the best parts about chilly winter days is getting to stay inside where it's warm and cozy. However, after too many days of staying inside, the house can start to feel a little *too* cozy. That's when it's fun to pick up a book! Reading takes you on adventures outside your house. And you don't have to worry about the weather.

Book nooks are especially nice on the days when you might feel tired of being stuck inside. And they don't take any special materials or space. You can use what you already have around the house. Making a book nook is like sending yourself an invitation: "Hey! Come over here and read with me!"

WHAT YOU NEED:

blankets
pillows
lamp or reading light
favorite stuffed animal
bookshelf or basket
decorations, such as
    fairy lights, a paper
    banner, or posters

WHAT TO DO:

1. Choose a place for your book nook. You can create it in a corner of your bedroom, in a closet, or in a quiet corner of the living room, attic, or basement.
2. Place a large pillow on the floor to sit on. Arrange the blankets and other pillows so you can read comfortably.
3. If your book nook will have a lamp, place it so the light shines on the large sitting pillow.
4. Put your favorite books on the shelf or in the basket. You can also store a reading light and bookmarks in a basket.
5. If a grown-up says it's okay, add decorations on the walls.
6. Choose a book and cuddle up. Let the story take you to a far-off place.

BOOKS TO READ

PICTURE BOOKS:

Katy and the Big Snow
Bread and Jam for
    Frances
Make Way for Ducklings
Madeline
Miss Rumphius
Last Stop on Market
    Street
Martin's Big Words
Malala's Magic Pencil
The Honeybee

CHAPTER BOOKS:

Charlotte's Web
The Lion, the Witch
    and the Wardrobe
Mr. Popper's Penguins
Mrs. Piggle-Wiggle
Frog and Toad Are
    Friends
James and the Giant
    Peach
A Little Princess
A Bear Called
    Paddington

Beezus and Ramona
The Borrowers
Roll of Thunder, Hear
    My Cry
The Boy Who
    Harnessed the
    Wind, Young
    Readers Edition
Quest for the Tree
    Kangaroo

LOOK FOR LICHEN

In wintertime everything outside can seem bare and drab. The leaves are gone. The grass is brown. The flowers aren't in bloom. Does *everything* die in the winter?

In fact, all sorts of organisms thrive in the cold season. And winter is a perfect time to look for lichen! Lichen looks like a plant or moss, but it isn't. Lichen is an amazing combination of three organisms: algae, fungi, and yeast. Lichen lives on rocks and tree bark. It can live in the frigid polar regions, the dry desert regions, and the warm tropical regions. Lichen can be green, gray, yellow, orange, or red.

Little lichen plays an important role in nature. It provides food and soft nest material for birds, insects, and small mammals. It helps plants and even trees grow on and out of rocks. Lichen breaks down the rock and creates cracks in the stone. As the lichen grows, it traps dust and water inside the crack. This makes a little bit of soil. Then when a bird or the wind drops a seed into the crack, a plant or tree can grow there.

Go for a winter hike and look for colorful lichen. It will stand out in the midst of the drab winter scene.

February 4
Joshua Tree National Park

Orange, green, and blue lichen. I think it is crusty crustose.

WHAT TO DO:

1. Hike where there are rocks, fallen trees, or living trees.
2. Look for patches of green, gray, yellow, orange, or red growing on the rocks and tree bark.
3. Watch for places where plants have grown out of a rock.
4. Take pictures or draw the lichen you see in your nature journal.
5. Make notes about lichen type, color, and what it grows on.
6. Identify the type of lichen. Is it crustose, foliose, or fruticose? When you get home, find out its name. Record the name in your nature journal.
7. Look for new types of lichen each time you take a winter hike.

FOLIOSE   FRUTICOSE   CRUSTOSE

KINDS OF LICHEN

FOLIOSE
leafy
grows from one spot

FRUTICOSE
bushy
skinny tendrils
hangs down like a beard

CRUSTOSE
crusty
flat edges
looks painted on

CELEBRATE THE SOLSTICE

Winter solstice is the first day of winter in the northern hemisphere. It's also the shortest day of the year and the longest night of the year. After the winter solstice, the days grow longer. The nights get shorter until the summer solstice in June.

A long time ago, the winter solstice was a special day. It meant the cold, dark winter was wrapping up. If you only had fire for warmth and light through the dark winter, you'd look forward to the return of long, sunny days too!

Even though we have heaters and electric lights now, we can still celebrate the changing season. It feels good to look forward to spring's return when everything will grow again.

WAYS TO CELEBRATE THE WINTER SOLSTICE:

- Take a moonlit hike.
- Make a fire outside. Sit around it and enjoy its warmth.
- Eat a warm winter meal by candlelight.
- Hang a bird feeder for the birds to enjoy until winter is past.
- Pop popcorn and watch your favorite winter movie.
- Gather around the table for a night of playing games.
- Make mugs of tea and read a favorite wintery book together.

DEAR PEN PAL

Getting letters in the mail is wonderful! As a child, writing to my pen pals was one of my favorite things to do. I had a few pen pals who lived in different states. I never met them, but we got to know each other through letters. I liked learning about the ways our lives were different and similar.

FIND A PEN PAL:

- Ask adults if they know of a kid your age looking for a pen pal.

- Or ask a grown-up to help you look online for pen pal groups.

Safety Tip! Let your parents know who your pen pal will be before you write your first letter. Be sure to let them see the letters from your pen pal too.

WRITE YOUR PEN PAL:

- Start your letter by introducing yourself. Describe where you live and how many siblings you have. Describe your favorite things to do and other interesting things about yourself.

- Consider sending stickers, a drawing, or a photograph.

- Include some questions you'd like your pen pal to answer.

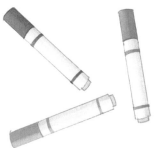

SNOW CASTLE

When it's snowy and cold outside, you might dream of sunny days at the beach. Well, guess what? You can still pull out your sand buckets and shovels and play! But instead of playing with sand, you'll build with snow. You can make a single snow castle or a whole snow village. Instead of seashells, decorate the castle with sticks, leaves, and acorns. When you're done, you'll have a beautiful snow castle scene to be proud of.

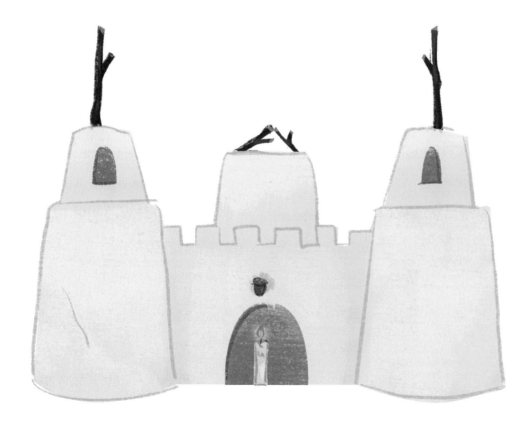

WHAT YOU NEED:

- wet and heavy snow that sticks together
- sand pails and molds (or plastic containers)
- sand shovels (or garden spades or large spoons)
- decorations, such as leaves, twigs, acorns, moss, rocks, or berries

WHAT TO DO:

1. Choose a building spot. Tamp down the snow flat and hard.
2. If you want to build a big castle, shovel snow into a large mound.
3. Gather snow from other parts of your yard to create the castle buildings. Leave lots of snow around your castle site.
4. For a large castle, use the pails or containers to create small buildings around and on top of the mound. Or build lots of castles to create a whole village.
5. Decorate your buildings.
6. At sunset, place tea light candles around your construction. Light them with an adult's help. Step back and admire your snow castle village in the glow of candlelight.

CREATE YOUR STATE

Did you know that every state has its own flower? In California, the state flower is the beautiful orange California poppy. In the spring, poppies cover the hills. And there are other kinds of state symbols. Every state has a state bird, animal, tree, rock or mineral, insect, fruit, fish, and a sport. Get to know your state as you get creative with its symbols by making a collage.

WHAT YOU NEED:

poster board
markers or colored
    pencils
printed pictures of state
    symbols
small objects related to
    the state symbols
glue

WHAT TO DO:

1. Title your poster with the name of your state. Write, use clipped letters from magazines, or shape letters with objects or craft supplies.
2. Add your state's motto or slogan to the poster.
3. Make a list of your state's symbols.
4. Create or find a representation of each symbol. You can draw pictures, print images from the internet, or use objects related to the symbol. For example, include a sticker from your state's NHL team if hockey is your state's sport. Or create a tree from pecan twigs and nuts if your state tree is the pecan tree. Or include a recipe for a dish made with your state's fruit. Have fun thinking of all the different ways to show the symbols.
5. Add the symbols to your poster.

POET PRACTICE: WINTER

This poem feels just right for winter. I like to think about being cozy and warm by the fire, drinking hot cocoa, and eating cookies on a wintry night. But I don't know that my mom would have let me have that for dinner! Would yours?

Make your favorite treat for your whole family and read them this poem.

Animal Crackers

Animal crackers and cocoa to drink,
That is the finest of suppers, I think;
When I'm grown up and can have what I please,
I think I shall always insist upon these.
What do you choose when you're offered a treat?
When Mother says, "What would you like best to eat?"
Is it waffles and syrup, or cinnamon toast?
It's cocoa and animals that I love most!
The kitchen's the coziest place that I know:
The kettle is singing, the stove is aglow,
And there in the twilight, how jolly to see
The cocoa and animals waiting for me.
Daddy and Mother dine later in state,
With Mary to cook for them, Susan to wait;
But they don't have nearly as much fun as I
Who eat in the kitchen with Nurse standing by;
And Daddy once said he would like to be me,
Having cocoa and animals once more for tea!

—Richard Hageman

ART ALIVE

One of my favorite artists is Vincent van Gogh. I love the bright colors and interesting patterns, lines, and details in his paintings. I had always thought Vincent's paintings were beautiful when I saw them in books or on a computer screen. But I will never forget the day I saw his paintings in real life.

Vincent's paintings took my breath away. They were so much brighter and more colorful than they looked in books. The colors seemed to jump right off the canvas!

When I got closer, I realized that Vincent used more colors than showed in the books. People's faces had stripes of green and orange and purple. The sky wasn't just blue. It was black and gray and gold and red.

And he piled the paint on so thick! In some places it came off the canvas in swirls and globs. He used all kinds of shapes, dots, and lines instead of just straight and simple brush strokes.

Seeing art straight from the artist's hand is special. I want you to have that same experience!

BEFORE YOU GO:

1. Think of an artist or artwork you like. If you don't know any, ask an adult to help you look for one in books or online.
2. When you find a work you like, find out whether any museums near you have pieces by that artist. If you're lucky, they might even have the specific painting, drawing, or sculpture you like best.
3. Learn what time period the work is from. Find out the name of the art style, such as impressionism, cubism, or Renaissance. This information will help you find the art in the museum.
4. Plan a trip to the museum.

AT THE MUSEUM:

1. Use a map or ask a worker to help you find the art or artist you came to see.
2. Observe the art up close. Then look from farther back. Do you notice any differences?
3. Look for details that are different in real life. Are the colors brighter? Is anything different from what you expected? Can you see sketch marks or brush marks or other clues about how the piece was made?
4. Look at other art nearby. Is it similar to the piece you came to see? Do you like it too?
5. Write down the names of other artists you like. Look them up when you get home.

FEED THE BIRDS

Many birds fly south for the winter. These birds eat worms, grubs, and other bugs from the ground or find food in the water. They need to fly south where the ground and water aren't frozen in the winter.

Other birds stay through the cold, dark winter. And they do just fine! These birds eat seeds, berries, and small insects. They can find that food in the snow and cold. But bird feeders can be an important part of their diet too. Plus, you can watch these feathered friends visit your feeder all winter long.

HANG A FEEDER:

1. Buy a bird feeder or make your own.
2. Hang your feeder from a tree or in front of a window.

WATCH THE FEEDER:

1. Watch what birds come to the feeder.
2. In your nature journal, write notes about the birds you see. What colors do you notice on them? How big are they? What time of day do they come?
3. Use a bird book to identify the different species.
4. Fill the bird feeder or make a new pine cone feeder every couple days. The birds will depend on you if wild winter food runs low.

EASY PINE CONE BIRD FEEDER

1. Coat a pine cone in peanut butter.
2. Roll the pine cone in birdseed.
3. Tie a string to the top.
4. Hang the feeder from a tree branch.

Popular Birds of North America

SNOW-WHITE CANVAS

Look outside your window on a snowy winter day. See all that white? Today it is your painting canvas!

Snow painting is different from the painting you're used to. It isn't done with brushes. And it doesn't make detailed pictures. This kind of art is wild and free.

Tip: Use lots of food coloring in the spray bottles. The more coloring you use, the brighter the "paint" color.

WHAT YOU NEED:

small spray bottles, one for each color

food coloring

COLOR MIXING

red + yellow = orange

blue + red = purple

yellow + blue = green

WHAT TO DO:

1. Fill the spray bottles with cool water.

2. Add one color of food coloring to each spray bottle. Red, yellow, and blue are primary colors. You can make one spray bottle for each of these three colors. Then layer them on the snow to create more colors. Or you can combine the primary colors in the spray bottles to create other colors.

3. Check with an adult about where in the yard to paint.

4. To the side of your main area, spray each color on the snow. Test the color and shape the spray makes.

5. Start creating. Try making a big rainbow, shapes, writing your name, or making polka dots of color. You can draw squares in the snow and create blocks of assorted colors. Or make another interesting design. Let your imagination run wild!

BAKE AND TAKE

Every winter my family turns our kitchen into a mini bakery. We make all kinds of treats. Then we deliver them to our friends and neighbors. We also like to decorate our packages for whatever holiday is close.

We like to be in the warm kitchen together, sampling the treats we make. But best of all is the delight on people's faces when we deliver a delicious gift.

WHAT TO DO:

1. Make a list of people to bake for. Besides friends and family, send some cheer to a family going through a challenging time or an elderly neighbor—even if you don't know them well.
2. Choose a recipe that will work well for that many people. If your list is large, choose an easy recipe that can be split many ways, such as cookies, brownies, or mini quick bread loaves. If you are baking for only a couple people, you could make something more difficult, like a pie. Or make something larger, like full-sized quick bread.
3. Go shopping for your ingredients. Don't forget any other supplies you need, such as cupcake papers, foil loaf pans, or parchment paper.
4. Bake when a grown-up says it's okay to make a mess in the kitchen.
5. When your baked goods have cooled, wrap them up. Add a note saying who they're from.
6. Deliver your delicious treats and some happiness!

SIMPLE FUDGE

What you need:

- **2 cups sugar**
- **1 teaspoon salt**
- **6 tablespoons unsalted butter**
- **1 cup heavy cream**
- **3 ½ cups mini marshmallows**
- **3 cups semisweet or white chocolate chips**
- **1 teaspoon pure vanilla extract**
- **½ cup crushed peppermint candy, nuts, or sprinkles (optional)**

What to do:

1. Line a 9 x 13-inch baking pan with two sheets of parchment paper. Crisscross the paper so each end overhangs a different side of the pan. Coat the paper with cooking spray.
2. Place the sugar, salt, butter, cream, and marshmallows in a heavy-bottomed saucepan. Cook over medium-high heat. Stir until butter and marshmallows are almost melted, 5 to 6 minutes. If the mixture starts to burn or bubble over, lower the heat.
3. Let the mixture come to a boil. Cook for about 5 more minutes, stirring often.
4. Remove from the stove. Add chips and vanilla. Stir until chips are totally melted.
5. Pour into the lined pan.
6. Let fudge cool at room temperature. It will take about 3 hours.
7. Use the edges of the paper to lift the fudge out of the pan. Place fudge on a cutting board and remove the parchment paper. Cut fudge into small shapes with cookie cutters. Or cut into squares.
8. Sprinkle evenly with crushed candy, nuts, or sprinkles.

ADAPTED FROM MARTHASTEWART.COM.

Tip: Recipes include a serving size. This tells you how many people the recipe will feed. You may need to double, triple, or even quadruple a recipe if you're baking for a lot of people. Be sure to buy enough ingredients and supplies.

OUTER SPACE ON THE CEILING

Find a seat and lean *way* back. As the lights dim, you see a galaxy of twinkles. The ceiling is covered with stars!

A planetarium is a special kind of theater where you can watch scenes of stars and planets on the ceiling. You can learn all about the study of outer space, called *astronomy*, at a planetarium.

WHAT TO DO:

1. Look for a planetarium in your area. You can often find them at colleges or in science museums.

2. Check the program schedule. Your planetarium might have nighttime programs for real-life stargazing. And some planetariums even have a humongous telescope available at certain times. You may be able to look through it on a clear night and see far into space.

3. At the planetarium, enjoy the show. Study the constellations on the ceiling above you.

4. Explore other exhibits in the planetarium or museum. There might be displays of meteors that have fallen from space to earth. Or there could be scales that tell you how much you weigh on different planets. What can you learn about astronomy?

5. If you want to keep learning about constellations, buy a star map at the gift shop. Or download a stargazing app on a grown-up's phone.

6. When you get home, wait for a clear night when the moon isn't too full. Go outside to see what constellations you can identify.

DESIGN A HABITAT DIORAMA

Make your own little world by creating a diorama of an animal habitat. Dioramas are fun to create because they can be made in many ways. All you need is some art supplies, a few nature materials to bring your scene to life, and a box. You can use a shoebox, carboard box with the flaps cut off, wooden box, or any small container.

Tip: Use flaps to make your paper pieces stand up. When cutting out a picture, leave a rectangle at the base of the image. Then fold the flap and glue it inside your box.

WHAT YOU NEED:

box

glue or tape

scissors

markers, crayons, or paint and
    brushes

white and colored cardstock paper

cotton balls

small nature materials, such as
    twigs, leaves, pebbles, and
    sand

mini animal figurines (optional)

WHAT TO DO:

1. Pick an animal you like or are interested in learning about. Investigate where that animal lives. What other animals and plants live there? What does the animal eat?

2. Create the background of your box. Use colors, paint, or paper to make the sky blue and the ground brown or green. You can also paste in pictures of mountains, trees, cliffs, or whatever landscape the habitat has. Glue on cotton-ball clouds and sand or pebble dirt. Let any paint and glue dry before moving to the next step.

3. Add landforms. Does the habitat have a river, boulders, or hills? Get creative by making shapes with foam, clay, paper plates, or other craft supplies. Blue plastic wrap makes great water because you can layer it over pebbles and drawings of fish.

4. Complete the landscape with plants. Draw them, print them, or create them with real plants. Twigs make great mini trees, and leaves can create bushes. If your animal is a plant eater, be sure to include some plants for its dinner.

5. Find a central spot to place your animal. Create a picture, print a photo, sculpt it from clay, or use a mini animal figurine.

6. Fill out the scene with other species. Does your animal eat other animals or insects? Does it live closely with another species? Choose a few other creatures to include.

7. Let the diorama dry.

8. Share your diorama with your family. Tell them what you have learned about the animal and its habitat and habits.

PARTY AROUND THE WORLD

Did you know you can travel around the world without ever getting on an airplane? You can experience the culture of another nation right in your own home by hosting an international party. Choose a country or region to focus on. Then plan a party of food, music, and other activities from that culture.

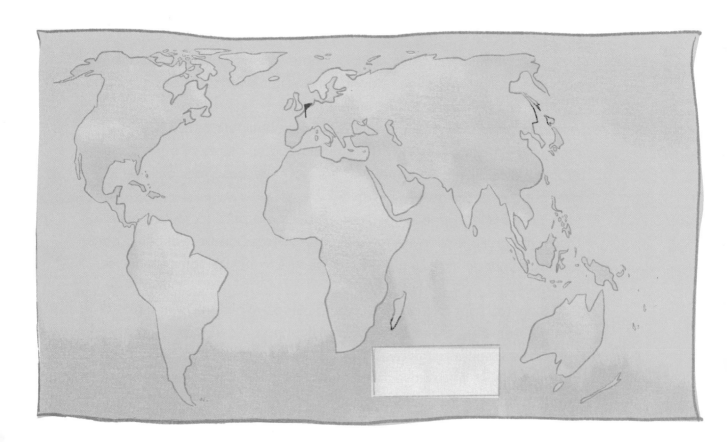

PLAN:

- Decide what part of the world you'll be traveling to.
- Choose a date and time for your party. Invite your friends.
- Research some snacks, meals, and desserts from that region. Use those to plan your menu.
- Find music from that country.
- Plan to make a craft or play a game that is popular in that country.
- Look for other things from the country to explore. You might watch a TV show, read a picture book, or enjoy a slideshow of photographs.

PREPARE:

- Make a shopping list. Include all the ingredients for your menu and any supplies you need for games or crafts.
- If you can, visit a specialty market that sells items from the country. Or look for your supplies in your neighborhood grocery store or an international market. If you can't find all your supplies in your town, order them online.
- Make any other preparations for the craft, game, or other activity.

PARTY:

- Before your guests arrive, prepare your food. Set the table for your friends.
- Play music from the country as you eat.
- Enjoy the other activities you planned.

MAKE STAMPED VALENTINES

The first party I planned for my friends was a Valentine's Day party. I was in fourth grade, and I invited friends over to decorate heart-shaped cookies and make valentines. After the party, I took the valentines to a home for the elderly. Sharing love is what Valentine's Day is all about.

Think of some people who will be cheered up by your stamped-heart art cards. Then gather your friends before Valentine's Day, make cards, and deliver them on February 14.

WHO NEEDS A VALENTINE?

elderly neighbors

kids in the hospital

families living at a shelter

kids living in foster homes

senior citizens at a nursing home

a person going through an illness or injury

WHAT YOU NEED:

Lego bricks

large potato

sharp knife

small, metal, heart-shaped cookie cutter

old sponges

old tablecloth or sheet

markers

pens

tempera paint

paper plates

paintbrushes

white and colored construction paper
   or cardstock

WHAT TO DO:

1. Use Legos to make a heart shape. Use a wider brick in the middle that sticks out the back. This will give your stamp a handle.
2. With an adult's help, cut the potato in half. Then press the cookie cutter into the potato's flesh. Cut the potato away outside the cookie cutter, about ¼ of an inch down. Remove the cookie cutter to see the raised heart in the potato.
3. Draw different sized hearts on the sponges. Cut out the shapes.
4. Cover the table with an old sheet or tablecloth. Set out the other supplies, and pour paint onto the paper plates.
5. Try the stamps on paper scraps. Try out different designs.
6. Use a combination of stamps and markers, or just stamps to make the cards. Lay the cards out to dry when you are done.
7. Write your name or a note inside the card.
8. On Valentine's Day, have an adult help you deliver the cards.

Tips:
- Use a thick layer of paint, or the paint will be clumpy and smudged.
- Experiment brushing paint on the stamps and dipping them in the paint to see which method you like best.
- Gently set your stamp on the paper, press firmly on it to transfer the paint, and pull the stamp up with one hand while you hold the paper down with the other hand.

START SEEDS

Even while it's still winter, gardeners dream of spring. They can't help thinking about the way the cold ground will warm up. And they imagine all the wonderful things they'll grow.

But the wait for the ground to thaw can be long. So many gardeners start their seeds ahead of time. They plant seeds in little cups or trays of soil in their houses. Once the seeds sprout and the weather warms, the gardener transfers the plants to the garden soil. These baby plants, called *seedlings*, grow fast because of their head start.

Are you dreaming of spring? Get a start on the season by growing seedlings.

February 27
My beans are
sprouting!

WHAT YOU NEED:

12 eggshell halves
1 teaspoon water
1 cup seed-starting
   soil

bottom half of
   cardboard egg
   carton
spoon

grass seeds, herb
   seeds, or flower
   seeds
spray bottle

WHAT TO DO:

1. Use soap and water to carefully clean the eggshells. Let them dry.
2. Bring your supplies outside on a bench or table. Or spread an old sheet on a table to catch stray dirt.
3. In a washable container, mix 1 teaspoon water into the soil.
4. Set the shells in the egg carton. With the spoon, fill them three-quarters full with the damp soil.
5. Gently press a couple of seeds into the soil in each shell. Follow the directions on the seed packet for how much soil should cover each kind of seed.
6. Leave the carton in or near a sunny window in the warmest room of your house.
7. Every couple of days, lightly spray the soil with water. Do not get it too wet.
8. Once your seedlings appear, remove the smallest plants. That gives the strongest seedlings more room to grow.
9. After there are a few sets of leaves on your seedlings, it's time to plant them in a bigger pot outside or in your garden. Gently break the bottom of the eggshell to make a hole for the roots to grow through.
10. Plant the seedling still in the shell in your pot or garden. The eggshell will give the seedling nutrients as it decomposes and the seedling grows!

WINTER SCAVENGING

Even in the coldest part of the year, you can find fresh fruit and vegetables at a farmers market or local farm. There are indoor farmers markets in cold places. In the southern parts of the country, farmers markets are open outside all year long.

In California where I live, oranges, grapefruit, lemons, persimmons, and avocados are in season during winter. Have you tried any of those fruits? All kinds of vegetables are in season too: broccoli, winter squash, turnips, and radishes. There are plenty of greens also: cabbage, collards, escarole, kale, and dandelion. Have you ever eaten any of those?

Discover what produce is in season where you live and try some.

WHAT TO DO:

1. Locate a farmers market or farm near you. Find out when it is open and plan a visit.
2. At the farmers market or farm, look for fresh fruits and vegetables.
3. If you don't recognize the produce you see, ask the farmer about them. Find out their names. Ask how to prepare and eat them.
4. Purchase a few fruits and vegetables to try.
5. Go home and share the food with your family!

- [ ] FLOWERS FOR KEEPS
- [ ] SPROUT A MIRACLE
- [ ] FOOD FORAGER
- [ ] MUD RUN FUN
- [ ] WILDFLOWER WALK
- [ ] BACKYARD PUMPKIN PATCH
- [ ] TAKE A NIGHT HIKE
- [ ] GARDEN SCAVENGER HUNT
- [ ] BE A CLOUD INTERPRETER
- [ ] NATIONAL PARK TOUR

ACTIVITIES FOR SPRING

- [ ] GO NUTTY FOR NETTLES
- [ ] DAY TRIP TO ANOTHER COUNTRY

"IS THE SPRING COMING?" HE SAID. "WHAT IS IT LIKE?" . . . "IT IS THE SUN SHINING ON THE RAIN AND THE RAIN FALLING ON THE SUNSHINE . . ." – FRANCES HODGSON BURNETT, *THE SECRET GARDEN*

- [ ] START AN ADVENTURE CLUB
- [ ] TAP A TREE AND MAKE MAPLE SYRUP

- [ ] GO BOULDERING
- [ ] TADPOLE TREASURE HUNT
- [ ] NATURE CLEANUP
- [ ] POET PRACTICE: SPRING
- [ ] GROW A SUNFLOWER HOUSE

- [ ] BEE A HIVE TOURIST
- [ ] NATURE DETECTIVE
- [ ] HONEY-TASTING PARTY
- [ ] WALK THROUGH HISTORY
- [ ] MONARCH WAYSTATION
- [ ] PLEIN AIR PAINTING

WILDFLOWER WALK

All across the United States every spring, wildflowers burst into bloom. In Texas, beautiful bluebonnets blanket the countryside. High in the mountains of Montana, over a thousand types of alpine wildflowers blossom. In New Hampshire, purple and pink lupines color the land. And in California, the hills—and even the deserts—are covered in bright orange poppies. Sometimes wildflowers bloom in such a large area that the colors can be seen in pictures that satellites take from space! This is called a super bloom.

Go on a wildflower walk to enjoy all the beautiful wildflowers that grow in your area.

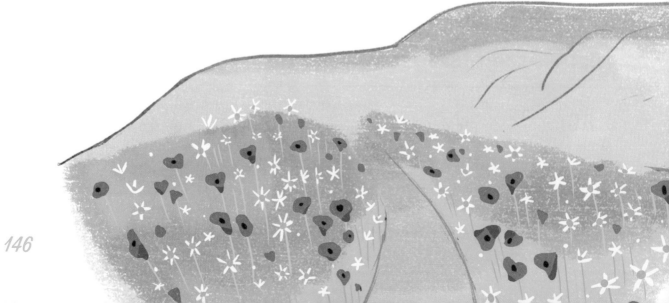

BEFORE YOU GO:

- Find out where wildflowers are blooming near your home. Look for fields of flowers while you're out driving. Or search online for "best wildflower blooms near ___" and insert your town's name.

- Check the weather forecast. Plan to go on a sunny day in the morning. Some wildflowers wilt when it gets hot. And some flowers will close on a rainy, gray, or windy day.

- Research the most common wildflowers in your area. It's more fun when you know what you're looking for.

- Pick a few favorite flowers and learn their names, color, and how to identify them.

- Make a checklist of local wildflowers to bring with you. Or buy a wildflower field guide for your area.

ON THE WALK:

- Stay on the path so you don't step on the wildflowers. If there is no path, walk around the flowers as much as you can. For example, keep to the edge of a field.

- Stop to look in tall grass and underneath other plants near the ground. You don't want to miss the smallest wildflowers.

- When you see a wildflower you can identify, check it off your list, circle it in your field guide, or write its name in your nature journal.

- If picking the flowers is allowed, make a wildflower bouquet. If picking is not allowed, take pictures, or draw your favorite wildflowers in your nature journal. Be sure to include their names.

PLEIN AIR PAINTING

Plein air painting is a fancy way of saying that you're taking your paints outside and painting from nature. More than one hundred years ago, a group of artists called the French Impressionists wanted to capture the effects of sunlight in their paintings. They made plein air painting popular. Since then, artists continue to love painting outdoors. They find a beautiful view and capture it with their paintbrushes.

PAINTING TIPS

- **Paint quickly.** The light outside can change in a short amount of time. Lighting affects the colors you see. Get the major color blocks on your paper as soon as you can.
- **Focus on shapes.** Paint the big shapes in the landscape first. Then add lines and other details.
- **Keep your painting dry.** Wipe off your brush after washing out a color. And don't use too much paint. You'll have a tough time carrying your work home if it's soaked through.
- **Be patient.** Painting from life, especially outside, is not easy. It takes time and practice to capture a view with your paintbrush.
- **Keep painting.** Revisit the same spot and paint at other times of day and in other seasons. You'll be amazed how different the landscape and your paintings will be!

WHAT YOU NEED:

- easel and canvas, clipboard and art paper, or sketchbook
- blanket or towel for sitting if you won't be standing at an easel
- pencil
- watercolors or acrylic paints
- paint palette or a plastic plate
- paintbrushes in a few sizes
- small container of water with a lid
- napkins or rag for drying brushes or mopping up spills
- sunscreen, a hat, or an umbrella stand

WHAT TO DO:

1. Find a beautiful outdoor location to paint in. You want a good view to capture.
2. Walk around the location to find your favorite view. You can paint a whole big landscape. Or you can paint a more focused view, like a tree or building.
3. Put up your easel or spread out your blanket.
4. Make some sketches of what you'd like to paint. Use them to decide exactly what you'll paint.
5. Set out your painting supplies.
6. Determine what colors you'll use.
7. Paint.

MUD RUN FUN

Mud runs are races that include running along trails, climbing over walls, carrying heavy loads, crawling on your stomach, jumping across ditches, and slogging through gigantic mud puddles.

Many mud runs are for adults, but there are special mud run races just for kids. While you may not be able to run the race with an adult, you can train for your races together. And a mud run is something you have to train for!

Find a mud run race near you and sign up. Make sure you have a few months to train before the race.

TRAIN TO RUN:

1. Learn how many miles the race will be. Walk that distance in your neighborhood or a nearby park.
2. After you know how far you must go, begin running part of the distance. Run farther each time until you can run the whole route.
3. Practice running on rough terrain like dirt trails.

TRAIN FOR THE OBSTACLES:

1. Find out what kind of obstacles will be in the race. What will you need to do to pass them?
2. To build strength, do push-ups, sit-ups, and jumping jacks. Practice jumping rope and planking your body. If you don't know how to do these exercises, ask an adult to help you learn.
3. Practice passing obstacles by climbing over and under benches or picnic tables, climbing trees, crossing the monkey bars at the park, and crawling in the grass on your stomach. You might even build a practice obstacle course in your yard. You just need equipment you can go over, under, around, and through. (Ask a grown-up what you can use before building your own course.)
4. After a couple of months of training, you'll be ready for the race.

GO TO THE RACE:

1. Wear old clothes, socks, and running shoes. Wear lightweight, breathable fabrics that won't become heavy when wet.
2. Bring two towels. You'll want one to wipe off right after the race. You'll use the second towel to dry off after you've gotten your turn to wash with water. Pack clean underwear, socks, shorts, shirt, and shoes. Bring a trash bag for your muddy clothes.
3. Have fun running the race!

FOOD FORAGER

A long time ago, almost everyone collected wild plants, nuts, and berries to eat. Native Americans were especially good at knowing all the plants in their area. They were experts at finding wild-grown food and just the right plant to use as medicine for all sorts of health problems. Searching for food in nature is called *foraging*.

Even though we find our food at the grocery store now, foraging is a neat skill to have. Pretend to be a clever forager from the past and learn to identify edible wild plants. (*Edible* means that you can eat it!) And who knows, the next time you're hungry in the wild, you might feel really smart as you munch on a good find along the trail.

Safety Tip! Never taste a plant unless you are 100 percent sure what it is. Some poisonous plants look similar to safe plants.

BEFORE YOU GO:

- Learn the edible plants that grow in your area. Search online, get an edible plants field guide, or sign up for a foraging class with an expert.

- Find out which parts of the plants are edible.

- Research the dangerous plants in your area. Make sure you can identify them easily.

ON YOUR FORAGE OUTING:

- Forage in a clean area. Avoid locations near a road with traffic fumes and areas that have been sprayed with pesticides.

- Harvest only the edible pieces so the plant can keep growing.

- Collect only as much as you will eat.

- Keep notes in your nature journal. Track the edible plants you see. Include pictures, drawings, and plant names.

WHEN YOU RETURN HOME:

- Find out the best way to prepare your foraged plants. Some are best dried and used for tea. Others can be eaten raw in a salad or juiced. Some are delicious cooked into all sorts of meals.

- Eat what you have gathered.

COMMON EDIBLE PLANTS IN THE WILD

dandelion
miner's lettuce
nasturtium
wild mustard
wood sorrel
wild radish
chickweed
plantain

GO NUTTY FOR NETTLES

Stinging nettles are a green that grows in the wild. Their leaves are jagged, like a saw. They're also covered with tiny hairs that sting if they touch your skin. If you cook them or dry them, however, they lose their sting. And then you can eat them!

Nettles are not only delicious, but they are also good for your body. They have nutrients your bones and blood need. They help your body get rid of toxic materials. And they can soothe swelling. Common ways to enjoy them are nettle tea, sautéed and mixed into eggs or pasta, or blended into soups, smoothies, and sauces.

Nettles are also great in a nutty sauce called pesto. Spread pesto on crusty bread or pizza or swirl into pasta.

Tip: Stinging nettles grow in many parts of the United States. Learn to identify them and forage them yourself. Or buy them from a farmers market. Just make sure you wear gloves when you handle them.

NETTLE PESTO

What you need:

- **¼ cup pine nuts**
- **3–4 cups raw stinging nettles**
- **2–3 medium garlic cloves**
- **¼ cup extra-virgin olive oil**
- **2 teaspoons lemon juice**
- **½ teaspoon salt**
- **¼ teaspoon pepper**
- **¼ cup grated fresh Parmesan cheese**
- **food processor or blender**

What to do:

1. Bring a large pot of water to boil.
2. While the water heats, toast the pine nuts. Place the nuts in a small skillet on medium-low heat. Stir and cook for about 3 minutes, until the nuts turn golden brown. Remove from the stove. Place in a bowl to cool.
3. Fill a large bowl with ice water.
4. When the water in the pot is boiling, use tongs to place the nettles with stems in the pot. Boil for 1 ½ minutes.
5. Remove nettles from the pot. Plunge them into the ice water.
6. Place the nettles on a clean, dry kitchen towel. Pull the leaves and small stems from the largest stems. Throw the large stems away.
7. Wrap the towel around the nettles and wring them over a sink. You'll now have about 1 cup of nettles.
8. Place the nettles, pine nuts, and all the other ingredients in a food processor. Pulse until mixed together but not totally smooth.
9. Scrape the pesto out of the food processor. Eat fresh or store in a sealed jar in the refrigerator.

ADAPTED FROM FEASTINGATHOME.COM.

TADPOLE TREASURE HUNT

Nature overflows with new life in the spring. Wildflowers bloom, leaves bud from trees, birds lay eggs in nests, and creeks and ponds fill with squirmy, round tadpoles.

One time my family found a pond with thousands and thousands of tadpoles. We put our fingers into the water and scooped up handfuls of tiny, swimming tadpoles! About a month later, we returned to the same place. As soon as we got close to the pond, the ground beneath our feet seemed to move. It was thousands of tiny frogs jumping through the grass toward the pond!

WHAT TO DO:

1. Find a creek or pond nearby. If it's a creek, look for a shallow place where the water moves slowly.
2. Look for tadpoles in areas that are murky or full of algae. Tadpoles eat algae.
3. Scoop up some tadpoles with a net, plastic bowl, or glass jar.
4. Observe the tadpoles for a few minutes. What color are they? Can you see through their skin? Can you see the beginnings of frog legs?
5. Return them to the water and keep watching. How do they move? Do they seem to notice the other tadpoles? Where do they like to hide?
6. Come back and see the tadpoles when they are frogs. If the tadpoles already have legs, come back in a week. If they don't have legs yet, come back in a couple of weeks or up to a month later.
7. Catch a frog and study its markings. Try to identify the species with a field guide or online search.

March 26

O'neill Park

I think we saw one million bajillion tadpoles today. There were so many that they looked like black clouds in the water. And they are slippery!

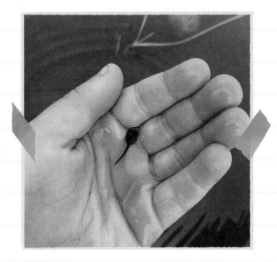

TAP A TREE AND MAKE MAPLE SYRUP

Do you love to drizzle maple syrup over your pancakes or waffles? I do! Did you know that you're actually pouring tree sap on your food? Yep. Maple syrup is tree sap that has been boiled down until it's thick, gooey, and delicious!

Most maple syrup comes from sugar maple trees. These trees make the most and the sweetest sap. But other trees can also make sap for syrup, including sycamores, box elders, black walnuts, butternuts, and birches.

Besides sap, you also need the right weather to make syrup. Sap runs when there are freezing nights and warmer days. This means sap is harvested in late winter and early spring.

If your region has the right kind of trees and weather, you can make your own maple syrup.

Tip: It takes about a gallon of sap to make a half cup of syrup.

WHAT YOU NEED:

- **power drill with a sharp bit (and an adult)**
- **hammer**
- **spout made for tree tapping**
- **lidded sap bucket**
- **large lidded food container**
- **large, heavy-bottomed pot**
- **stainless steel fine-mesh strainer**
- **clean glass bottle and lid**
- **metal funnel**

Tip: If tree tapping isn't possible where you live, you can still enjoy the process. Watch videos online about tapping trees and making syrup. Or read about it in a book. The novel *Little House in the Big Woods* has a whole chapter that describes how to make maple syrup.

WHAT TO DO:

1. Find a sap tree that's at least 10 inches across.
2. With an adult's help, drill a hole two inches deep in the tree. The hole should be slanted slightly upward.
3. Use a hammer to gently tap the spout into the hole. Hang the bucket from the spout.
4. Collect the sap daily. Pour it into a large, lidded container. Keep the container in the fridge until you have collected enough sap to make syrup.
5. Pour the sap through the strainer and into a large, heavy-bottomed pot. On the stovetop, bring the sap to a boil. Then turn down the heat to keep a very low boil. Boil for about 1 hour. Watch carefully to be sure the syrup doesn't boil over. Turn down the heat if needed.
6. Rinse the glass bottle with warm water. Then use the metal funnel to pour the hot syrup into the empty glass bottle. Put the lid on right away. You can keep an unopened bottle of syrup for two years. An opened bottle will stay fresh in the fridge for one year.

GROW A SUNFLOWER HOUSE

Can you imagine a playhouse with flower walls, a grass-carpet floor, and a ceiling of blue sky? That's a sunflower house!

WHAT YOU NEED:

an area of your yard that gets
    full sun all day long and is
    at least five feet wide and
    five feet across
string
garden spade
watering can or hose

sunflower seeds

seeds for giant sunflowers:
    American Giant, Sunzilla,
    Skyscraper, Paul Bunyan, or
    Mammoth

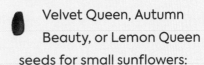

seeds for medium sunflowers:
    Velvet Queen, Autumn
    Beauty, or Lemon Queen

seeds for small sunflowers:

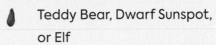

    Teddy Bear, Dwarf Sunspot,
    or Elf

WHAT TO DO:

1. Use string to outline a large square or circle shape for your flower house. Make sure it is large enough for you and a sibling or friend to sit inside.
2. Dig a shallow trench along the outline. Be sure to leave a large gap for the door.
3. Plant the seeds of the giant sunflowers in the trench. Plant the seeds every 6 to 12 inches to make thick walls. Follow the directions on the seed packages for how deep to plant the seeds.
4. Plant the seeds for the medium and small flowers between the seeds of the giant flowers.
5. Water your seeds according to the directions on the seed packets.
6. Water your seeds each day and watch the flowers grow.
7. Be patient. It will take 2 to 3 months for your sunflower walls to grow tall and for the flowers to bloom.
8. Once your sunflower house is in full bloom, lay a blanket on the ground. Enjoy your beautiful, sunny flower house.

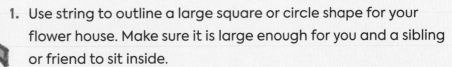

START AN ADVENTURE CLUB

My family has been part of an adventure club for twelve years. Every week we meet with our friends and go on an adventure. Often, we hike. We also visit tide pools and museums, read books together, and take classes. One time we went on a tour at an olive-packing factory. Exploring together is the best!

Ask an adult to help you create your own adventure club.

PLAN YOUR CLUB:

1. Create a list of friends to invite.
2. Decide who will go on the adventures. Will your friends' whole families come along? Or will your parent take you and your friends out? Ask your grown-up what they prefer.

PLAN YOUR FIRST ADVENTURE:

1. Pick a location close to where you live.
2. Choose an activity for the adventure. Will you go hiking, learn something new from an expert, tour a museum, or something else?
3. Get approval for the place and activity from your parent or sponsoring adult.
4. Invite your friends to the first adventure. Tell them where it is, what time to arrive, and what to bring.
5. After the adventure, send an email to your friends. Tell them that you'd like to adventure with them again and invite them to join the adventure club. Then start planning your next adventure!

MUSEUM

April 24

Winter Creek Trail

We went on a 3-mile hike with our adventure club today.

We saw a Western Toad, a kestrel, an Acorn Woodpecker, and bobcat tracks!

SPROUT A MIRACLE

Isn't it fun to watch things grow? Seeing a hard, dry seed turn into a living, green plant is a chance to watch one of God's creation miracles.

When you plant a seed, you usually don't see anything for a while. Then suddenly a tiny shoot pops up above the dirt. But a lot has happened before then. The seed has split open. And it has sent down roots to anchor it in the ground. You can watch this amazing underground process by sprouting a plant with water instead of dirt.

Keep Growing! For another growing project, sprout beans. Choose a few dried beans or bean seeds. Use large beans, such as kidney beans, lima beans, or butter beans. Place the beans or seeds on a damp paper towel. Then seal them in a Ziploc bag. Put the bag in a warm, dry place. On top of the fridge is a good spot. After a week, check for sprouts!

WHAT YOU NEED:

small sweet potato or an
    avocado pit, washed and
    dried
four toothpicks
clear glass jar

WHAT TO DO:

1. Stick one toothpick in each side of the avocado pit or potato.
2. Fill a large glass jar with water. Leave room at the top for the avocado pit or potato.
3. Position the avocado pit with the flatter, rougher end down. Or position the potato with the pointed end down.
4. Place the pit or potato in the water. The toothpicks will rest on the mouth of the jar. You may need to adjust the amount of water in the jar so that the pit or potato is under water right up to the top of the jar.
5. Add water each week to keep the jar full.
6. Watch the miracle of new life sprout and grow!

TAKE A NIGHT HIKE

Nature comes alive in new ways in the dark. Strange sounds echo from animals that come out after sundown. Sweet smells sail on the breeze from plants that release scents at night. Other growing things smell stronger in the cooler air. Follow your favorite local trail by moonlight and experience a familiar place in a fresh way.

WHAT TO BRING:

layers of clothing for
the cool evening
temperatures
water bottle and snacks
headlamp or flashlight
with a red light
setting or covered
with red plastic wrap
glow sticks

BEFORE YOU HIKE:

- Pick a trail that is easy and familiar. Also choose a trail where the moon's light will shine on the path.
- Check the hours of the trail. Some trails close after dark.
- Plan to hike on a night when the moon is full for the most light.
- Be prepared to come across wildlife. Many animals are most active at night. Know what to do if you meet them.
- Plan to hike with a small group. Never hike alone.
- Let an adult who's staying home know where you're going. Make plans to tell them you've returned by a certain time.
- Attach glow sticks to everyone's backpack. Or wear them on wrists or around necks. The glow sticks will help you see the other hikers on the trail.

ON THE HIKE:

- Hike without lights (except the glow sticks). It can take about a half hour for your eyes to adjust to the moonlight. If you must use a headlamp or flashlight, use the red light setting. Red light will help you keep your night vision. And keep your light out of everyone's faces. Their eyes will have to adjust all over again.
- Hike slowly. Move with care since you can't see the trail as well as you are used to.
- Always stay with the group.
- If you are in an area without large predators, talk in a whisper. You will see more wildlife if you don't scare creatures away before you get close. If you are hiking where bears or mountain lions live, talk loudly instead.
- Every few minutes, stop to observe. What do you hear? How does the trail look different? Do you smell anything new?

AFTER THE HIKE:

- Let the grown-up at home know you got back safely.
- Write about your night hike in your nature journal. What things were different from hiking during the daytime? List any animals you saw. Make a sketch of what the trail looked like in the moonlight.

GO BOULDERING

Bouldering is a kind of rock climbing. Bouldering doesn't use ropes or harnesses. Instead, you rely on your own strength, flexibility, balance, and brain power. You're probably already great at bouldering, even if you don't know it. That's because kids are great at climbing, and they do it often.

You can practice bouldering at a rock-climbing gym. But bouldering is the most fun outside. It's an exciting challenge to use the natural cracks and ridges of the rocks to climb up and over them.

You don't need special equipment to start bouldering. But if you keep practicing and start climbing higher boulders, a little gear might help. Rock-climbing shoes will give your feet better grip. Crash pads will soften your landing if you fall.

WHAT YOU NEED:

- closed-toe shoes with good tread
- long pants
- gloves if the rocks are rough

WHAT TO DO:

1. Find a place near you with boulders to climb.
2. Start by climbing smaller rocks.
3. Before you climb a rock, study it. Look for cracks or bumps to use as hand and toe holds. Find routes up and down the rock.
4. Climb slowly. If you feel stuck, stay calm. Look and feel around for a new path up. If you really get stuck, go down the way you came.
5. Have an adult stand below for help if you need it. That's called *spotting*.
6. Challenge yourself to climb more difficult rocks as you gain experience.
7. Watch videos online of experienced boulderers. You'll be inspired to keep climbing!

NATIONAL PARK TOUR

I was ten years old the first time I visited a national park. Yosemite National Park in California is home to some of the world's biggest trees. The trees are so huge that when one fell over a road, the park cut a tunnel through it. Cars can still drive through this tree tunnel today.

And all these years later, those trees I visited as a girl are still there. That's because they are protected in a national park. The government has created national parks because these areas contain land that is beautiful, majestic, and unique. National parks preserve that beauty. People come from all around the world to see them.

There are sixty-three national parks across the United States. Many states have at least one national park. Learn what you can about a park from home. Then plan a visit.

LEARN:

1. Choose a national park near where you live. Or select one your family would like to visit on vacation.
2. Find out the history of the park. When did it become a national park? What makes it special?
3. Learn about the famous places or parts of the park.
4. Research the habitat. What animals live there? What plants and trees grow there?

PLAN:

1. Make a checklist of animals you might see in the park.
2. Print out a map of the park. Create an itinerary of the top three places you'd most like to visit.
3. Find one special adventure you'd like to try. You might choose a challenging hike, a visit to a beaver pond, or a river rafting experience. Draw a picture of the adventure to help you remember it as your special goal.
4. Ask a grown-up if your family can make plans to visit the park sometime in the next year. Share your trip ideas with someone in your family.

NATURE CLEANUP

Spending time in nature is one of my favorite ways to relax. But I hate it when I am out in a pretty spot and find trash on the ground or graffiti sprayed on rocks. It's easy to get angry at the people who don't care for nature or don't practice "leave no trace." But I decided my family should do something helpful instead of just being mad. So I always bring a plastic bag and disposable gloves for picking up trash when we find it.

We also sign up for volunteer days at our favorite nature spots. Cleaning up trash is a wonderful way to care for God's creation and keep it nice for everyone to enjoy.

WHAT TO DO:

1. Choose a nature spot you visit often.
2. Find out if this spot has trash cleanup days.
3. If your spot has scheduled cleanup days, join one. If your spot doesn't have scheduled days, plan a time to clean up with your family or friends.
4. On cleanup day, bring trash bags and disposable gloves. Fill up a bag or two with trash.
5. To clean graffiti, ask an adult to help you use a paint remover and scrub brush.
6. After you clean up, enjoy the beauty of your favorite spot.

POET PRACTICE: SPRING

Y ou can never be sure what the weather will be like in springtime. Sometimes the sun is out and the trees are full of blossoms. Then a surprise snowstorm comes. Spring flowers poke their stems through the snow. Often, we're longing for sunshine, but the days are full of rain.

That's why this poem about the weather feels right for springtime. Read it aloud and enjoy the sounds of the words jumbling in your mouth. Practice saying it a few times. Before you know it, you'll have it memorized.

Whether the Weather

Whether the weather be fine
Or whether the weather be not,
Whether the weather be cold
Or whether the weather be hot,
We'll weather the weather
Whatever the weather,
Whether we like it or not.
—traditional English rhyme

MONARCH WAYSTATION

Did you know that butterflies travel three thousand miles each year? Every spring, millions of monarch butterflies migrate back from central Mexico to the United States and Canada as the weather becomes warmer. They travel up to 100 miles each day, and one way to help them on their long journey is to plant a waystation. A monarch waystation is a place along the way for

the butterflies to rest, lay their eggs, drink nectar, and recover before continuing on.

One spring we planted milkweed plants in our backyard. Milkweed is a perfect plant for a monarch waystation because milkweed is the only plant butterflies lay eggs on.

It was thrilling to find monarch eggs on the milkweed leaves. Soon we saw the teeny caterpillars crawling around, munching on the leaves. Monarch caterpillars love milkweed leaves and begin eating them as soon as they can.

Next, beautiful, soft, green chrysalises appeared around our yard. They hung on potted plants and in the rose bush. They even dangled from the side of the house.

After a couple of weeks, the first chrysalis split open. We watched the butterfly emerge. It hung and dried its crumpled wings for several hours. Then it stretched, fluttered, and flew away. What an incredible thing to witness! All because we planted some milkweed for the butterflies to rest on during their long trip north.

WHAT YOU NEED:

- **6 or more milkweed plants**
- **an area of yard to plant in or a pot for each plant**
- **bright flowers planted nearby**
- **magnifying glass**

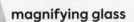

WHAT TO DO:

1. In early March, plant the milkweed. Plant in your yard near bright flowers that will attract the butterflies. If you don't have a yard or enough space, put the milkweed in pots and add other pots of blooming flowers near them.

2. Water your milkweed plants lightly each day for a week. Then only water if the ground becomes very dry.

3. Watch for the monarchs to find your milkweed. Use the magnifying glass to look for tiny light-colored eggs. They are usually on the underside of the milkweed leaves.

4. A week after you first see eggs, start checking for caterpillars. Watch them grow!

5. Next, look for green chrysalises in the area around the milkweed. Without touching, examine them with the magnifying glass.

6. Check back every day. Watch as the chrysalises change from green to clear. When can you see the black-and-orange wing pattern inside?

7. The butterfly will come out 9 to 14 days after a caterpillar makes a chrysalis. Check each chrysalis often. Then watch the butterfly dry its wings and flutter away.

BE A CLOUD INTERPRETER

ave you ever watched the clouds? Maybe you looked for shapes in them, like dinosaurs, birds, or castles. Or maybe you watched thunderclouds roll in with flashing lightning. We know that thunderclouds mean a storm. But did you know that all clouds give clues about the weather? Learn to interpret the clouds and be prepared when you're out in nature.

> *Tip:* The higher the clouds, the clearer the weather will be.

WHAT TO DO:

1. Go outside and look at the clouds.
2. In your nature journal, draw a picture of the clouds. Use "Types of Clouds" to identify the cloud. Label the cloud with its name.
3. Make a weather forecast based on the type of cloud.
4. Keep an eye on the weather for the next day and log it in your journal. Did your prediction come true? If it didn't, compare your drawing to the images in "Types of Clouds." Is there another type of cloud it could have been?
5. Continue tracking the clouds you see. Practice making weather predictions and recording whether your forecast was right. And remember, weather forecasters for the news aren't always right either. There's a lot more to the weather than just clouds. And sometimes those things change, and the weather doesn't do what you expect.

TYPES OF CLOUDS

Cirrus

Weather Forecast: fair now; storm and temperature change later

Stratus

Weather Forecast: light rain when appearing during the day; clear day when appearing overnight

Cumulus

Weather Forecast: heavy rain when clumped together; good weather when spread out

Cirrocumulus

Weather Forecast: fair; cold

Cumulonimbus

Weather Forecast: thunderstorm

Nimbostratus

Weather Forecast: snow or rain for several hours

GARDEN SCAVENGER HUNT

Can you find a sneezewort yarrow? How about a snapdragon or a bird of paradise? There are so many kinds of strange and beautiful plants. And some of them have pretty silly names! Explore the colorful world of plants with a trip to an arboretum or botanical garden.

April 12

Sweetwood

Botanical Garden

I finished the

scavenger hunt first

with my final find:

this cypress tree.

BEFORE YOU GO:

1. Visit the garden's website. Find out what plants are blooming.
2. Choose 5 to 10 plants from the list. Include plants from all over the arboretum.
3. Find pictures of the plants on your list.
4. Make a scavenger hunt checklist with the names and photos of the plants. Put the paper on a clipboard. You'll need to write while you walk around.

AT THE ARBORETUM:

1. Get a map. Try to locate the areas with the plants on your list.
2. Visit each spot and search for the plants.
3. When you find one, check it off your list.
4. If you have a hard time finding any of the plants, ask a worker for help.
5. Choose a few favorite plants. Add their names and drawings to your nature journal.

Orchid

A diverse and widespread family of flowering plants

Tulip

The flowers are usually large, brightly colored.

Colors: red, pink, yellow, or white.

WALK THROUGH HISTORY

One of my favorite neighbors when I was young was Mrs. Shipley. She was an elderly woman who had lived in our town her whole life. When Mrs. Shipley was a girl, a horse and wagon delivered milk in the morning. She remembered when the library was built. She liked to walk there to check out books just like I did. But back then, the streets were hard, packed dirt instead of pavement. Mrs. Shipley loved to tell me stories about our town, and I loved to listen.

Every city and town has a story. Discover some of the amazing things that have happened in your town.

WHAT TO DO:

- Visit your town's museum or historical society.

- Choose a famous person or place in your town. Make a scrapbook of the person's or place's lifetime.

- Find the oldest buildings in your town. Visit them and go inside if you can. If the building is a house, look up whether the owners participate in historical tours.

- Visit your town's first cemetery. Read the names and messages on the graves. Choose a few people who interest you. Try to find out more about their lives and the town when they were alive. Use what you learned to write a fictional story about them.

- Talk to one of your town's older residents. Ask them to tell you what the town was like when they were young.

- Look up old pictures of your town online. Make a model of the old main street or one of the well-known buildings. Use Legos or build the model out of cardboard.

- Make a scrapbook of your town's history. Include your own illustrations or copies of old photographs.

- Make a video tour of some of the historical places around town. Share information about when they were built and who built them. Talk about what they have been used for over the years.

FINDING OLD RECORDS AND PHOTOS

Library: Libraries have lots of information about local history, including books, photographs, old newspapers, and even objects. Tell a librarian what information you're looking for. He will have several ideas of good places to search.

Historical society: Many towns have a special organization that keeps local history safe. They may run a museum or share information on their website. You can also contact the society for help. Just email them with a message about what you're researching.

Newspaper company: If your town has had the same newspaper for a long time, they might have copies of old issues or a website with a photo database.

Internet search: Search for your town's name and "local history." Or do a search for a person's or place's name and your town's name.

BEE A HIVE TOURIST

Honeybees are some of the most important creatures on earth. They help flowers, fruits, and vegetables grow by pollinating them. We need bees!

That's why it's great that beekeeping has become popular. Beekeepers make hives for bees in safe places. They also harvest honey. Learn all about the work of bees and beekeepers by touring a hive farm. And if you're lucky, you'll get to try fresh honey!

WHAT TO DO:

1. Search online for a beekeepers association in your area. Find one that gives classes or tours. Plan a visit with your family or adventure club.

2. On the day of your tour, wear pants and closed-toe shoes. Don't put fragrance on your body, including scented lotion. You don't want the bees to like you too much. When you get to the farm, you will be given a bee suit and hat.

3. Listen to the beekeeper's instructions. There are important ways to stay safe and not get stung.

4. Watch as the beekeeper shows you the beehives. This is where the bees live, make the honey, and raise baby bees. The keeper will show you the special tools she uses to harvest honey from the hives. The keeper will also tell you some of the amazing things bees do. She'll also share what you can do to help the honeybee population continue to grow.

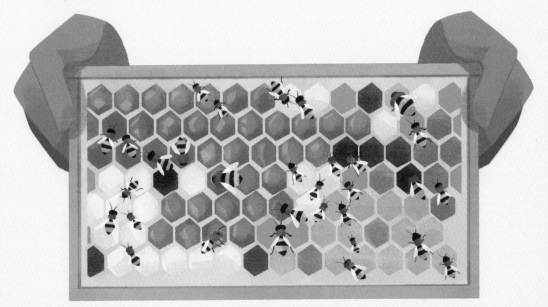

HONEY-TASTING PARTY

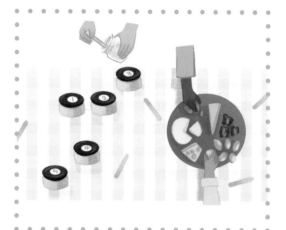

Did you know that bees are the only insects that produce food that humans eat? Did you know that there are over three hundred flavors of honey in the United States? Bees make all that honey from the nectar of flowers. Honey's color and flavor depend on which flowers the bees gathered nectar from to make the honey.

Honey tasting is a delicious experiment. Share the sweetness with your friends by inviting them for a tasting party.

HONEY FACTS

- A bee produces about one teaspoon of honey in its lifetime.
- To make a pound of honey, a bee colony gathers nectar from about two million flowers.
- A sealed jar of honey can last thousands of years.
- Honey has been used as medicine for thousands of years.

WHAT YOU NEED:

- **old tablecloth or sheet**
- **samples of honey from a farmers market, local farm, or beekeeper**
    - a light, mild flavor
    - a medium flavor
    - a dark, intense flavor
    - other interesting flavors (optional)
- **popsicle sticks or plastic spoons**
- **snacks that pair well with honey**
    - fruit, such as grapes, apples, or pears
    - nuts, such as almonds or walnuts
    - cheese, such as sharp cheddar or brie
    - crackers or baguette slices
- **plates and napkins**
- **pitcher of water and cups**
- **voting sheet for guests to mark their most and least favorite types of honey**
- **pencils or pens**

WHAT TO DO:

1. Before your guests arrive, cover the honey labels with paper. Number each jar. Your friends will vote without knowing the kinds of honey.
2. Put an old tablecloth or sheet on the table. It will get sticky!
3. Set the table with all your honey-tasting supplies.
4. When your friends have arrived, taste the first type of honey together. Don't tell them the flavor!
5. Ask everyone to guess what kind of flowers the bees used to make the honey.
6. Taste the other flavors one by one. Guess the flavor of each.
7. Direct everyone to mark the voting sheet.
8. Add up the votes. Announce which numbered honey jar is the most and least popular.
9. Remove the papers from the honey jars. Reveal the flavor of each jar.
10. Share some honey facts with your friends.

NATURE DETECTIVE

Animals are sneaky. They creep around your yard at night. They run across the trail when no one is around. They scout for food and water in the dim dusk hours. But you can discover what animals are up to. You just need to decode the clues of their tracks.

TIPS FOR IDENTIFYING TRACKS

Deer, fox, and coyote walk in a zig zag pattern.

Bears, skunks, and racoons are waddlers. They leave tracks of four prints.

Rabbits, mice, and squirrels are hoppers. Their prints are deeper in back where their feet push off to jump.

WHAT TO DO:

1. Get a local animal tracking guide from the internet, library, bookstore, or nature center. Look at all the shapes and sizes of animal tracks.
2. Take the guide with you to hunt for tracks. Good places to look are the beach, on a dirt trail after it rains, in a spot of soft soil in your yard, or in the snow.
3. When you find a track, examine it.

    What size is it?
    What shape is it?
    How many toes can you count?
    Does it have nails or claws?
    Did the toes or the heel make a deeper print?

4. Use the guide to help you identify the tracks.
5. If you find a path of tracks, follow it for more clues.

    Does the path zig zag or go straight?
    Does the animal have two feet or four feet?
    Where do the tracks lead? Where do you think the animal was going?

Soon you'll be able to identify common tracks without even using the guide. You'll be an expert nature detective!

BACKYARD PUMPKIN PATCH

One spring my mom planted pumpkins in our backyard. She planted big ones and small ones. It was fun to watch them grow through the summer. We tried to guess how big they would grow. Which ones would grow into giants big enough for us to sit on? Which ones would be little baby pumpkins we could hold in our hands?

By the time fall came around, we had a pile of pumpkins of assorted sizes, shapes, and colors. Some were bright orange. Others were pale yellow or deep red. There were plenty of medium-sized ones, just right for carving into jack-o'-lanterns. But my favorites were the huge ones. We had to roll them from the backyard because they were too heavy to carry.

Tip: Look for a seed that grows a "bush" pumpkin if you don't have a lot of room. This plant will grow in a smaller space than most pumpkin vines, which sprawl out.

CHOOSE YOUR PUMPKIN SEEDS:

1. Decide whether you want big pumpkins, medium pumpkins, or small pumpkins. You can also choose different colors.
2. Find out the right time to plant your seeds. The bigger the pumpkin, the longer it will take to grow. Find the "days to maturity" on the seed packet. Then look up when the first frost usually happens where you live. Find the day of the first frost on a calendar, then count backward the number of days to maturity. The day you end on is when you should plant your seeds. If you're growing more than one type of pumpkin, you'll plant the large pumpkins earlier than the small pumpkins.

CHOOSE WHERE TO PLANT:

1. Choose a spot that gets sun all day.
2. Make little hills of dirt for your pumpkin seeds. This helps the ground drain water. It also allows the long pumpkin vines to trail onto the ground.
3. Follow the planting directions on the seed packet and put your seeds in the ground.

CARE FOR YOUR PUMPKINS:

1. Water your pumpkin plants, following the directions on the seed packet. Be sure not to overwater them. The leaves might look wilted in the heat of the day, even when the soil is moist. Just wait until evening. They'll perk right back up.
2. Feed your pumpkins with a garden fertilizer.
3. When the fruit starts to appear, put a layer of straw under the pumpkins. This helps the fruit hold on to moisture. The straw also helps the pumpkins to not get a discolored spot.

HARVEST YOUR PUMPKINS:

1. Your pumpkins are ready to harvest when their rinds are hard and they are the color described on the seed packet. Before harvesting, double-check the days to maturity and when you planted them.
2. Ask an adult to help you cut the pumpkin from the vine. Leave a few inches of stem attached to the pumpkin.
3. Cook with your pumpkin, carve it, or decorate with it.

FLOWERS FOR KEEPS

People have been preserving flowers since the days of ancient Egypt. The Egyptians decorated tombs with dried flowers. They also used dried flowers in perfumes and cosmetics. In England in the 1800s, people often saved flowers from a special day by pressing them between the pages of a book. Then they laid the flowers on pieces of silk or lace and framed them behind glass.

PLANTS FOR PRESSING

The best flowers for pressing lay flat and hold their color. They also have thin petals, stalks, and centers.

cosmos	daisies	ferns
pansies	violets	moss
wild mustard	shrub roses	eucalyptus
delphinium	Queen Anne's lace	seaweed

WHAT YOU NEED:

large books
newspaper or cardstock
freshly picked flowers and
    plants

Tip: Press your flowers as soon as you pick them, so they look fresh.

WHAT TO DO:

1. Open a big, heavy book to the middle.
2. Lay several pieces of newspaper or cardstock in the book. Neatly arrange the flowers and plants on the paper. Make sure none of the flowers are touching.
3. Lay a few more sheets of paper on top of the flowers. Close the book.
4. Put more books on top to add weight.
5. After a week, gently open the book. Check whether your flowers are dry. If they are not fully dry, close the book and let them press for another week.
6. When the flowers are dry, gently remove them with tweezers.
7. Make something beautiful with your flowers.

    Make framed art: Arrange the flowers on a sheet of thick paper. Put them in a frame.

    Add them to your nature journal: Use clear packing tape or contact paper to attach flowers to the pages of your journal. Add the flower names and when and where you found them.

    Make bookmarks or cards: Cut a piece of cardstock to the size you want for your bookmark or card. Then cut a piece of contact paper a little smaller than the cardstock. Lay out the flowers facedown on the contact paper. Press the contact paper and flowers onto the cardstock. Add an encouraging message.

DAY TRIP TO ANOTHER COUNTRY

Most cities have ethnic neighborhoods. These are areas where people from a specific culture live, work, and have fun. There's Chinatown in San Francisco, the Polish Triangle in Chicago, Greek Town in Baltimore, and Little Italy in New York City. In these neighborhoods, restaurants serve that culture's foods. Markets sell spices, clothing, and newspapers in other languages. On special holidays, parades strut through the streets. And there are other special events to celebrate the culture. It's like visiting another country without getting on a plane.

WHAT TO DO:

1. Find an ethnic neighborhood near you. Ask an adult if they know of one. Or search online for "ethnic neighborhood" and the name of your city or state.
2. Plan a trip. Try to go on a festival or cultural day. There will be even more to see and do.
3. When you arrive, enjoy a meal at a restaurant. Try some new foods!
4. Visit the shops and markets. What is different from the stores you are used to? Ask the workers about the items that are new to you. What are they? How are they made?
5. Look for a museum or cultural center. Stop inside and learn more about this place and its people.
6. Try to learn a few words in the culture's language. Your waiter will love it when you say "thank you" in their native tongue.

ACKNOWLEDGMENTS

For the past thirteen years, I have adventured every week with my friends. We hike, explore, discover, dream, and learn together. They are the inspiration for this book.

Thank you, Adventure Club mamas and kids, for being my companions on this journey. Your enthusiasm for adventure makes me want to share our adventures with the whole world. So I did!

Aaron, thank you for saying yes with me to another book, for picking up the slack when I have a crazy deadline, and never minding when I fall asleep on the couch because I stayed up too late writing. You're the very best.

James, William, Lilly, and Davy, you help me be a more adventurous mom. Thank you! I love you all.

To my amazing team at Tommy Nelson, thank you for helping me write my first children's book! It's a lifelong dream come true. There was a steep learning curve, but you were with me every step of the way and I am so grateful for each one of you.

ABOUT THE AUTHOR

Greta Eskridge is author of the book *Adventuring Together: How to Create Connections and Make Lasting Memories With Your Kids*. Greta is passionate about creating connection, protecting children, and chasing adventure. Greta shares her message of joyful, connected parenting on her website, her Instagram feed, and at speaking engagements around the country. Greta, her husband, Aaron, and their four kids make their home in sunny Southern California.